Cambridge Elementary Classics

# LIVIANA

Cambridge University Press
Fetter Lane, London

*New York*
*Bombay, Calcutta, Madras*
*Toronto*
Macmillan

*Tokyo*
Maruzen Company, Ltd

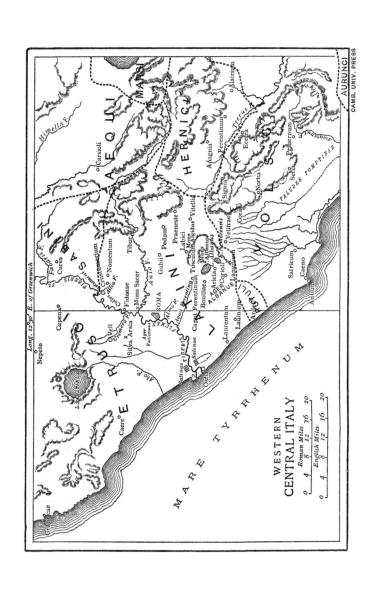

WESTERN
CENTRAL ITALY

Roman Miles
0    4    8    12    16    20

English Miles
0    4    8    12    16    20

AURUNCI
CAMB. UNIV. PRESS

MARE TYRRHENUM

Long. 12°30' E. of Greenwich

ETRURIA

AEQUI

MARSI

HERNICI

VOLSCI

LATINI

SABINI

ROMA

Tibur

Praeneste

Gabii

Pedum

Labici

Mons Algidus

Tusculum

Vitellia

Signia

Ferentinum

Anagnia

Norba

Setia

PALUDES POMPTINAE

Carsioli

Nomentum

Crustumerium

Fidenae

Mons Sacer

Cures

Eretum

Capena

Veii

Nepete

Caere

Fregenae

Ostia

Laurentum

Lavinium

Ardea

Antium

Satricum

Caeno

Velitrae

Cora

Aricia

Bovillae

Alba Longa

ALBANUS

Corioli

Lanuvium

Ferentinum

Tellenae

Ficana

Silva Arsia

Cremera

Ager Vaticanus

Fossae Cluiliae

Ferentinum

Ecetra

Fabraterna

Fregellae

Fabrateria

Frusino

Treius F.

Verulae

Aletrium

Himella F.

Allia F.

Anio F.

Tiberis F.

Nar F.

Aefula

# LIVIANA

## A SECOND YEAR LATIN READER & WRITER BASED ON LIVY I & II

*By*

ELEANOR PURDIE, Ph.D.

FOR TWENTY-FIVE YEARS HEAD CLASSICAL
TUTOR AT THE CHELTENHAM LADIES' COLLEGE

CAMBRIDGE: AT THE
UNIVERSITY   PRESS
1930

CAMBRIDGE UNIVERSITY PRESS
Cambridge, New York, Melbourne, Madrid, Cape Town,
Singapore, São Paulo, Delhi, Tokyo, Mexico City

Cambridge University Press
The Edinburgh Building, Cambridge CB2 8RU, UK

Published in the United States of America by
Cambridge University Press, New York

www.cambridge.org
Information on this title: www.cambridge.org/9780521239486

First published 1924
Reprinted 1927, 1930
First paperback edition 2011

*A catalogue record for this publication is available from the British Library*

ISBN 978-0-521-23948-6 Paperback

# PREFACE

THE object of this book is to provide for the second year of Latin continuous reading matter which has been carefully graded to proceed parallel with the learning and practice of the 'second year constructions.' The number of these that can be grasped in one year will depend of course upon the capacity of the class and the amount of time given to the subject. Some may be unable to go farther than chapter 15 and will not be able to include in this year's work dependent questions and exclamations. Others may get as far as chapter 19, but will not contrive to reach the chapters on the various types of conditional sentence. A more rapid class still will manage to cope not only with these but even with the mysteries of the double use of the gerund-adjective. The treatment of these two last subjects is not intended to be exhaustive, but to give the pupil some initiation at least into these indispensable constructions.

A synopsis is given of the constructions dealt with in the exercises. The *A* exercises are recapitulatory as regards constructions but generally reproduce the vocabulary of the chapter to which they are parallel. The *B* exercises are intended for the practice of the new constructions. All are on retranslation lines, but some adaptation of the text is invariably required.

It is intended that the exercises shall not be

attempted until the vocabulary of the corresponding chapter has been adequately assimilated, and
that they shall then be done from memory. To
ensure this no English into Latin vocabulary is
supplied: in its place there is given a reference to
the chapter in which the necessary word or phrase
occurs for the first time. The few words required
that do not occur in the text are supplied in the
vocabulary.

Only ten of the passages chosen are from Book I:
the other fourteen are drawn from Book II, which
on the whole will probably be less familiar and
therefore more interesting. The original text has
necessarily been greatly simplified, and here and
there a few sentences have been interpolated in
order to illustrate the desired constructions. A few
pieces from Ovid's *Fasti*, illustrative of some of the
stories told in the text, have been added for the
sake of teachers who may welcome the opportunity
of reading a little verse with intelligent pupils in
their second year. The new words required for the
understanding of the Ovid passages are given in a
separate vocabulary.

The prose vocabulary may at first sight seem too
extensive, but three considerations should be borne
in mind. The pupil will already be familiar with
many of the words, which, for the sake of com-
pleteness, have been given in full in the vocabulary.
Further it is not essential that all words should be
known from the *English* side: the number of these
which should be assimilated can be settled by the

teacher according to the capacity of the class and with due reference to the knowledge requisite for the English into Latin exercises. Finally the importance of the acquisition of a fairly comprehensive vocabulary can hardly be overestimated, particularly in days when the power to translate accurately at sight is recognized, at any rate in the case of pupils of merely average ability, as of much greater importance than the power of turning English into Latin. All teachers who have been responsible of late years for preparing pupils for 'first' and 'second' examinations in Latin must have noticed how greatly the demand for 'sight translation,' and that often of real difficulty, has increased, and how sadly the pupil's power to meet this demand is diminished by the want of a basic vocabulary with which he or she is thoroughly familiar.

Notes are given where special help seems necessary: other necessary information will be found in the vocabularies. With these aids the pupil should generally be able to prepare the text without help from the teacher in advance.

The recommendations of the 'Joint Committee on the Unification and Simplification of Grammatical Terminology,' as set forth in the Report issued in 1911, have been followed without reservation: from this point of view, therefore, the book may be used with confidence in schools that have adopted the reformed terminology in all languages.

Quantities have only been marked in the text where they throw light on the meaning: but the necessary help towards correct pronunciation will be found in the vocabularies.

The knowledge presupposed before this book is begun may be summarized as follows: *Accidence.* Familiarity with all but the subjunctive forms of the regular conjugations and of *sum, possum, volo, nolo, malo, eo, fero*: the declension of nouns and adjectives: the formation of adverbs and the comparison of adjectives and adverbs: *is, ille, hic, ipse* and the personal and relative pronouns. *Syntax.* The most important of the elementary case usages, including the rules for place and time, and the commonest prepositions and their uses: the distinction between active, passive and deponent verbs: the use of the relative pronoun: the ordinary ways of asking simple non-dependent questions: the indicative uses of the commonest conjunctions, *e.g. ubi, postquam, quamquam, quod* and *quia, si, dum.*

Subjunctive forms are not required till chapter 7, and then only the present and past tenses: the subjunctive tenses of completed action are not introduced till chapters 13 and 14. Pronouns other than those included in the first year scheme and anomalous adjectives like *totus* and *unus* may be learnt as they occur in the text.

I must conclude by expressing my acknowledgments to Prof. Conway's illuminating edition, in the Pitt Press Series, of Livy II, and my sincere gratitude to several of my former colleagues on the staff of the Ladies' College, Cheltenham, for invaluable help in criticism and encouragement of my efforts to produce this little book.

# CONTENTS

# LIVIANA

In primo libro operis sui narrat Livius multas fabulas de regibus antiquis qui Romae regnavisse dicuntur. Primum narrat de origine urbis Romae, quae a Romulo condita est, postea de ratione mirabili mortis illius. Tempestas enim subito coorta 5 est cum magno fragore tonitribusque, et Romulus nimbo denso opertus esse dicitur nec postea in terris fuisse. Deinde, dum cives desiderio regis solliciti sunt, homo quidam, Proculus Iulius, in medium progressus, 'Romulus,' inquit, 'parens 10 huius urbis, hodie primā luce de caelo delapsus mihi occurrit, et verba gravissima de Romā, capite orbis terrarum olim futurā, locutus sublimis abiit.' Proculo haec de immortalitate Romuli et urbis fortunā nuntianti facile credebat plebs 15 Romana, nec tantum quantum antea de morte eius dolebant.

Romulo successit Numa Pompilius, vir ei dissimillimus. Omnium enim operum eius maximum fuit tutela pacis per omne regni tempus. 20

Ita duo deinceps reges, Romulus bello, Numa pace, civitatem auxerunt.

The combat of the Horatii and the Curiatii in the reign of 2
Tullus Hostilius.

Tertius rex Romanus fuit Tullus Hostilius, qui non solum dissimilis erat proximo regi sed ferocior

etiam quam Romulus. Dum ille regnat, multa
bella gesta sunt, ex quibus bellum Albanum claris-
5 simum factum est pugnā trigeminorum qui *forte*
in duobus exercitibus tum erant, nec virtute nec
aetate dispares, Horatii Curiatiique appellati. Ex
eventu huius pugnae pendebat imperium.

Armis igitur captis trigemini in medium inter
10 duas acies processerunt. Consederant utrimque
pro castris duo exercitus, periculi expertes sed non
curae; ubi vero primo concursu increpuerunt arma
micantesque fulserunt gladii, horror ingens spec-
tantes perstrinxit. Consertis deinde manibus duo
15 Romani, alius super alium, volneratis tribus Al-
banis, exspirantes corruerunt. Unus autem, quem
tres Curiatii circumvenerant, integer fuit et adversus singulos ferox. Fugā igitur captā prohibuit eos
simul omnes adgredi, et iam *aliquantum spatii* ex
20 eo loco ubi pugnaverant aufugerat, *cum* respiciens
magnis intervallis sequentes eos *vidit.* In proxi-
mum hostem magno impetu rediit, tum illo occiso
alterum quoque consecutus interfecit. Iamque singuli supererant, sed nec spe nec viribus erant
25 pares: alter enim, nondum volneratus, victoriā bis
reportatā ferocissimus erat: alter fessum volnere,
fessum cursu corpus trahens, et summā maestitiā
adfectus quia fratres iam interfecti erant, victori
hosti obiectus est. Tum Romanus exsultans 'Duos'
30 inquit, 'fratrum iam occīdi, tertius mox ad inferos
eos sequetur.' Deinde gladium ei superne defixit
iacentemque spoliavit.

The reign of Ancus Marcius.    **3**

Mortuo Tullo Hostilio, primo breve interregnum erat; postea Ancum Marcium regem populus creavit. Is Numae Pompilii regis nepos erat, filiā eius ortus. Qui ubi regnare coepit, sperabant cives avo eum similem futurum esse; finitimi autem populi 5 eum spernebant, quia putabant Romanum regem pigrum inter sacella et aras regnum acturum esse. *Re verā* medium erat in Anco ingenium, et Numae et Romulo simile. Intellexit igitur temptari a Latinis patientiam suam temporaque Tullo regi 10 aptiora esse quam Numae. Itaque, demandatā curā sacrorum sacerdotibus exercituque novo conscripto, profectus urbem Latinorum vi cepit, *secutus*que morem regum priorum multitudinem omnem Romam traduxit. Deinde Marte incerto 15 aliquamdiu pugnavit. Denique omnibus copiis conisus acie primum hostes vicit, deinde, postquam Romam rediit, multa milia Latinorum in civitatem accepit. Sic urbem Romam auxit Ancus Marcius. 20

Ei non successerunt filii eius, sed vir quidam, Lucumo nomine, cuius pater Corintho olim ob seditiones profugus in urbe Etruscā consederat et, uxore ibi in matrimonium ductā, duos filios genuerat. Nomina his Lucumo atque Arruns 25 fuerunt.

**4** Lucumo becomes L. Tarquinius Priscus, the fifth king of Rome.

Arruns prior quam pater mortuus est; Lucumo superfuit patri, omnium bonorum heres, et his divitiis elatus altiora petere in animo habebat. Incitabat quoque eum uxor eius, Tanaquil, quae,
5 summo loco ipsa orta, haud facile sinebat domum in quam innupserat humiliorem esse domo in quā erat nata. Constituit igitur Romam migrare, *rata* ibi in novo populo futurum esse locum forti ac strenuo viro. Itaque sublatis rebus Romam mi-
10 graverunt: ubi paene ad urbem venerunt, Tanaquil *ex* aquilā quādam laetum augurium se accepisse rata, virum amplexa excelsa et alta sperare iussit. Has spes cogitationesque secum portantes urbem ingressi sunt, domicilioque ibi comparato nomen
15 falsum, L. Tarquinium Priscum, ediderunt. Tum benignis verbis, cōmitate, beneficiis omnes sibi conciliabant, donec in regiam quoque de L. Tarquinio fama perlata est. Denique, regis amicitiā comparatā, tutor etiam liberis testamento eius est
20 institutus. Mortuo autem rege tutorem infidelem se exhibuit. Orationem enim apud plebem habuisse dicitur: *se* Romam cum coniuge ac fortunis omnibus commigrasse et ibi sub optimo magistro, Anco rege, Romana iura, Romanos ritus didicisse: ob-
25 sequio et observantiā *in* regem cum omnibus *certasse*, benignitate erga alios cum rege *ipso*. His verbis permotus ingenti consensu populus L. Tarquinium Priscum regnare iussit.

The rise of Servius Tullius.    **5**

Multos annos regnavit **L.** Tarquinius Priscus, multa bella gessit, multa pacis opera vel inchoavit vel perfecit; dicitur infima urbis loca circa forum aliasque convalles, quia ex planis locis haud facile evehebant aquas cives, cloacis *fastigio* in Tiberim 5 ductis siccavisse.

Dum ille regnat, ferunt in capite pueri cuiusdam, cui *Servio Tullio* fuit nomen, in regiā dormientis flammam apparuisse multorum in conspectu: magno igitur clamore ad rem tam mirabilem orto 10 excitos esse reges; voluisse quendam familiarium flammam restinguere, reginam autem vetuisse, negavisse flammam puerum laesuram esse; mox cum somno flammam quoque abisse. Tum, abducto in secretum Tarquinio, Tanaquil 'Videsne' 15 inquit, 'hunc puerum, quem tam humili cultu educamus? Pro certo habē hunc futurum esse olim lumen rebus nostris dubiis praesidiumque regiae adflictae. Necesse est igitur omni indulgentiā nostrā eum nutrire.' Inde puerum *ut* 20 filium suum *habere* coeperunt reges et artibus liberalibus erudire; postea, ubi manifestum erat eum iuvenem ingenii vere regii esse, filiam suam ei desponderunt.

Duodequadragesimo anno ex quo regnare coe- 25 perat Tarquinius, magno apud omnes cives honore erat gener eius, Servius Tullius. Tum Anci filii duo, quos antea narravimus a patrio regno tutoris fraude pulsos esse, querebantur sine dubio regna-

30 turum esse olim Servium: ne ab Tarquinio quidem
ad se rediturum regnum: dedecus id fore et domui
suae et omnibus Romanis. Ferro igitur id dedecus
arcere et regi insidias parare statuerunt: sperabant
enim illo occiso facile fore sibi regnum patrium
35 occupare.

**6** Plot against Tarquinius Priscus: the guile displayed by
Tanaquil.

Duo pastores igitur, homines ferocissimi, ad hoc
facinus delecti in vestibulo regiae, dum rixam
simulant, omnes regis apparitores in se convertunt.
Inde, ubi ambo regem appellarunt clamorque
5 eorum penitus in regiam pervenit, vocati ad regem
pergunt. Primo certatim alter alteri obstrepunt.
Coerciti ab lictore et invicem dicere iussi tandem
obloqui desistunt; unus, sicut inter eos convenerat,
rem narrare coepit. Intentus in eum se rex avertit:
10 tum alter elatam securim in caput deicit relictoque
in volnere telo ambo se foras proripiunt. Tarquinium morientem ubi ei qui circa erant exceperunt,
sceleris ministros, dum fugere conantur, compre-
hendunt lictores. Tanaquil autem, femina dolorum
15 peritissima, Anci filios regnum occupare sic prohibuit. Servium enim Tullium celeriter accitum
his verbis adlocuta est: 'Tuum est,' inquit, 'Servi,
si vir es, regnum, non eorum qui pessimum facinus
fecerunt. Erige te, deosque duces sequere, qui
20 clarum fore hoc caput divino quondam circumfuso
igni portenderunt.' Deinde ex superiore parte
aedium per fenestras populum quoque adlocuta est.

Iussit eos bono animo esse: *sopitum esse regem*
subito ictu; ferrum haud alte in corpus descen-
disse; inspectum esse volnus absterso sanguine; 25
omnia salubria esse; regem ipsum eos mox visuros;
interim omnia Servio Tullio eum commisisse;
illum iura redditurum et cetera regis munera *ex-*
*secuturum.* Tum Servius cum trabeā et lictoribus
prodiit ac in sede regiā sedens alia ipse decernebat, 30
de aliis consulturum se regem simulabat. Itaque
per aliquot dies, quamquam Tarquinius iam ex-
spiraverat, morte eius celatā suas opes firmavit.
Tum demum, comploratione in regiā ortā, res
patefacta est. Anci liberi, postquam vivere regem 35
et tantas esse opes Servii nuntiatum est, in exsilium abierunt.

**Plot against Servius Tullius by Lucius, son of Tarquinius 7
Priscus, who had by that time married his younger daughter.**

Servius Tullius, quamquam se regem esse iam-
dudum simulabat, tamen a populo nondum rex
factus erat; postea autem, ubi agros ex hostibus
captos viritim divisit, eo consilio ut voluntatem
plebis sibi conciliaret, paene omnium consensu 5
rex est declaratus.

Publica opera multa perfecit Servius, et privatis
quoque consiliis opes suas firmare conatus est;
duas enim filias, ut Tarquinii filios amicos sibi
redderet, iuvenibus regiis, Lucio atque Arrunti 10
Tarquiniis, in matrimonium dedit. Deiectus est
autem hac spe amicitiae; nam ex his filiabus eius
Tullia minor, femina violentissima, multis et

secretis sermonibus habitis cum Lucio, sororis
15 marito, qui iuvenis erat animi ardentis, mox ad
atrox scelus eum induxit. Postquam enim Tullia
maior, uxor Lucii, et Arruns Tarquinius, Tulliae
minoris maritus, interfecti sunt, nuptiis Lucio
iuncta est. Tum vero in dies *infestior* Tullii
20 senectus esse coepit. Iam enim ab alio ad aliud
scelus spectabat mulier: nec noctu nec interdiu
virum quiescere passa est, ne praeterita parri-
cidia gratuita essent. 'Noli,' inquit, 'sperare
potius quam habere regnum. Si tu is es cui
25 nuptam me esse puto, et virum et regem te appello.
Di te et patris imago et domus regia et in domo
regium solium creant vocantque regem. Noli tu
ignavus esse.'

Tandem, his verbis uxoris incitatus, in forum
30 cum agmine armatorum inrupit L. Tarquinius, et,
omnibus terrore perculsis, in regiā sede pro curiā
sedens patres ad regem Tarquinium citari iussit.
Qui ubi convenerunt, orationem vehementem
contra Servium habuit Tarquinius: *servum* eum
35 servāque natum post mortem indignam parentis
sui occupasse regnum a muliere *datum*. Huic
orationi ubi intervenit Servius, trepido nuntio
excitatus, extemplo magnā voce, 'Quid hoc'
inquit, 'est, Tarquini? Quā tu audaciā *me vivo*
40 ausus es patres convocare aut in sede meā con-
sidere?' Ad haec ferociter respondit Tarquinius
se patris sui tenere sedem; filium enim se esse regis
et regni heredem. Tum medium arripuit Servium,
elatumque e curiā in inferiorem partem per gradus

deiecit, inde in curiam rediit. Facta est fuga regis 45
apparitorum atque comitum: ipse ab eis interfectus est qui, a Tarquinio missi, fugientem eum
consecuti erant.

### Arrogance shown by Tarquinius Superbus. 8

Inde L. Tarquinius regnare coepit, cui Superbo
cognomen datum est, quia socerum sepeliri pro-
hibuerat. Armatis corpus suum circumsaepsit:
necesse enim ei erat regnum metu tutari. Primores
patrum, quos Servii rebus favisse credebat, inter- 5
fecit, numerumque eorum ita imminuit, neque
senatum de omnibus rebus consuluit sed suis
ipsius consiliis rempublicam administravit; bellum,
pacem, foedera, societates per se ipse fecit diremit-
que. 10
Iam magna erat Tarquinii auctoritas inter primores Latinorum, *cum* in diem certam ad lucum
Ferentinae *indictus est* conventus eorum. Convenerunt illi primā luce frequentes: Tarquinius
diem quidem servavit, sed vix ante solis occasum 15
advenit. Iam propter moram diuturnam incensa
erat ira primorum, praecipue Turni Aricini, qui
ferociter in absentem Tarquinium erat invectus.
'Haud mirum est' inquit, 'Superbo datum esse ei
Romae cognomen. Principibus enim longe a domo 20
excitis ipse, qui concilium indixit, non adest. Si
me audietis, domos abibitis: neque observabitis
diem concilii quam ipse qui indixit non observavit.'
Orationi eius intervenit ipse Tarquinius, qui, ut se
purgaret, dixit se moratum esse ut patrem et 25

filium in gratiam reconciliaret: ad posterum diem
necesse esse omnia differri. Turnus, postquam in
regem multa increpuit, ex concilio abiit. Extemplo
Tarquinius, quia hanc rem aegerrime ferebat,
30 mortem Turno machinabatur. Oblato igitur falso
crimine innocentem eum oppressit. Servo enim
Turni auro corrupto magnum numerum gladiorum
noctu in deversorium eius clam inferri iussit. Tum
Tarquinius paulo ante lucem accitis ad se principi-
35 bus Latinis, 'Mora mea hesterna' inquit, '*saluti
fuit* et mihi et vobis. Dicitur ab Turno mihi et
primoribus populorum parari exitium: dicitur
gladiorum ingens numerus ad eum convectus esse,
ut Latinorum solus imperium teneat. Hinc mecum
40 ad Turnum venite omnes.' Postquam igitur ad
deversorium Turni se contulerunt, custodes eum
ex somno excitatum circumsteterunt: alii, com-
prehensis servis qui ob caritatem domini vim
parabant, gladios abditos ex omnibus locis dever-
45 sorii protraxerunt. Tum vero manifesta res est
visa iniectaeque Turno catenae. Confestim Latinorum concilio advocato indictā causā condemnatus est ille et, crate superne iniectā saxisque
congestis, in aquā Ferentinā demersus.

**9** Tarquinius Superbus sends two of his sons, accompanied
by a nephew, to consult the oracle at Delphi.

Tum Volscis bellum indixit Superbus atque,
urbe Suessā Pometiā vi captā multum pecuniae
adeptus constituit aedificare in monte Capitolino
Iovis templum, regni sui nominisque monumen-

tum, quod dignum esset et Iove, deum hominum- 5
que rege, et Romano imperio. Pecunia autem ex
praedā refecta vix ad fundamenta templi suffecit.
Tarquinius igitur, qui templum perficere multum
studebat, publicā quoque pecuniā ad id usus est.

Haec agenti Tarquinio portentum terribile visum 10
est: anguis ex columnā ligneā elapsus non solum
terrorem fugamque in regiā fecit sed ipsius quoque
regis animum curis anxiis implevit. Perterritus
igitur Delphos, ad clarissimum in terris oraculum,
mittere statuit filios duos, Titum et Arruntem, 15
sciscitatum. Comes eis additus est L. Iunius
Brutus, Tarquiniā, regis sorore, natus, qui, ut con-
temptu tutus esset neve ab avunculo, sicut frater
suus, interficeretur, specie stultitiae ex industriā
indutā, ne *Bruti* quidem cognomen abnuerat. Tum 20
ab Tarquiniis Delphos ductus aureum baculum
corneo inclusum donum Apollini tulisse dicitur,
effigiem ingenii sui. Postquam Delphos venerunt
iuvenes, patris mandatis perfectis, aliud responsum
ex deo his verbis quaesiverunt. 'Ad quem nos- 25
trum,' inquiunt, 'O Apollo, regnum Romanum
olim veniet?' Tum ex infimo specu vocem reddi-
tam esse ferunt: 'Imperium summum is Romae
habebit qui vestrum primus, O iuvenes, osculum
matri tulerit.' Quo responso accepto Titus et 30
Arruns sic inter se disputabant: 'Uter nostrum
prior cum Romam redierimus, matri osculum
dabit? Utri regnum dabitur?' Tandem vero,
quia rem ipsi decernere non poterant, 'Sorti'
inquiunt, 'rem permittemus; decernet Apollo.' 35

Brutus autem, vocem Apollinis *alio* spectare ratus,
simulavit se prolapsum cecidisse et terram osculo
sic contigit; intellexit enim communem matrem
omnium mortalium esse terram. Inde redierunt
40 Romam, ubi adversus Rutulos bellum summā vi
parabatur.

**10** The end of the kingship at Rome (510 B.C.).

Minimus ex tribus filiis regis erat Sextus Tarquinius, vir sicut pater sceleratissimus. Erat
quoque Tarquinius Collatinus quidam, nepos illius
Arruntis qui frater erat L. Tarquinii Prisci. Hic
5 in matrimonium duxerat Lucretiam, feminam
spectatissimam, quae Collatiae habitabat. Vir
autem eius cum rege et regiis iuvenibus aberat in
stativis circa Ardeam, urbem Rutulorum, quam
Romani obsidione premebant. Olim Lucretia, ubi
10 iniuria a Sexto Tarquinio ei inlata est, nuntio
ad Spurium Lucretium, patrem, et Collatinum,
virum, misso, oravit ut *cum singulis* fidelibus
*amicis* Collatiam venirent. 'Res atrox' inquit,
'incidit. Summā celeritate veniant pater et vir
15 meus.' Venit Sp. Lucretius cum Valerio, Collatinus cum cognato, L. Iunio Bruto. 'Equos' inquiunt, 'calcaribus concitemus ut quam celerrime
Collatiam adveniamus; Lucretia enim per nuntium
nos arcessivit.' Lucretiam maestam in cubiculo
20 sedentem inveniunt. Quae simul atque eis persuasit ut pollicerentur se poenas de Sexto sump-
turos, cultrum quem sub veste abditum habebat,

in corde defixit, prolapsaque in cultrum moribunda
cecidit. Conclamant vir paterque. Brutus, illis
luctu occupatis, cultrum ex volnere Lucretiae 25
extractum prae se tenens, 'Per hunc sanguinem,'
inquit, 'iuro me L. Tarquinium Superbum cum
sceleratā coniuge et omnibus liberis ferro ignique
vel aliā vi exsecuturum, nec illos nec alium quem-
quam Romae regnare passurum.' Cultrum deinde 30
Collatino tradit, inde Lucretio ac Valerio. Hi, ut
praeceptum erat, iurant, totique ab luctu in iram
versi Brutum ducem sequuntur. Elatum domo
Lucretiae corpus in forum deferunt concientque
homines. Omnes scelus regium ac vim queruntur: 35
movet eos simul patris maestitia, simul Bruti
oratio: reprehendebat enim lacrimas et inertes
querellas monebatque ut arma caperent adversus
gentem regiam. Armati, *duce Bruto*, Romam profecti sunt, et ubi eo venerunt, pavorem ubique ac 40
tumultum faciunt; itaque ex omnibus locis in
forum concurrunt homines. Ibi apud convocatum
populum orationem habuit Brutus de vi Sexti
Tarquinii et morte Lucretiae, de superbiā regis et
laboribus miseriisque plebis: *Romanos homines,* 45
victores omnium circa populorum, opifices ac
lapicidas pro bellatoribus esse *factos.* His verbis
incensae multitudini suasit ut imperium regi abro-
garet exsulesque esse iuberet L. Tarquinium et
uxorem et liberos. Tum Tarquinio Superbo, qui, 50
harum rerum nuntiis Ardeam in castra perlatis,
Romam festinaverat, clausae sunt portae ex-
siliumque indictum. Romae duo consules creati

sunt, L. Iunius Brutus, liberator urbis, et L.
55 Tarquinius Collatinus.

L. Tarquinius Superbus cum duobus filiis exsulatum Caere in Etruscos abiit: Sextus Tarquinius
Gabiis est interfectus.

**11** Lucius Tarquinius Collatinus resigns his consulship under
pressure.

Postquam expulsi sunt Tarquinii, nomen consulis alterius, quamquam nihil aliud offendit, in-
visum fuit civibus. Primum per totam civitatem
sermo est dissipatus ipsum nomen Tarquinii peri-
5 culosum esse libertati. Tum orationem apud
plebem ad contionem vocatam habuit Brutus.
'Non credit' inquit, 'populus Romanus solidam
libertatem reciperatam esse. Regium genus, regium nomen non solum in civitate sed etiam in
10 imperio est. Id obstat libertati. Hunc metum tu,
L. Tarquini, tuā voluntate remove. Te reges
eiecisse et meminimus et fatemur. Perfice beneficium tuum, aufer hinc regium nomen. Res tuas
non solum reddent cives tui, sed etiam, si quid
15 deest, munifice augebunt. Amicus abī, exonerā
civitatem metu.'

Collatinus primo prae admiratione huius tam
novae ac subitae rei nihil respondit; deinde loqui
incipientem eum primores civitatis circumsistunt;
20 orant obsecrantque ne Romae diutius mancat. Et
ceteri quidem minus eum movebant: postquam
vero socer eius, Sp. Lucretius, aetate ac dignitate
maior, ei suadere coepit ne civium consensui

resisteret, consul, nc postea privatus non solum
expelleretur sed etiam bona amitteret, abdicavit se ₂₅
consulatu, rebusque suis omnibus Lavinium trans-
latis a civitate discessit.  Brutus populo persuasit
ut imperaret ne quis Tarquiniae gentis Romae
relinqueretur.  Collcgam sibi creavit P. Valerium,
cuius auxilio reges eiecerat.                        ₃₀

Plot at Rome to restore the Tarquins.                **12**

Quamquam bellum a Tarquiniis imminere vix
cuiquam in dubio erat, id serius accidit quam
sperabant: ceterum, id quod non timebant, per
dolum ac proditionem paene amissa est libertas.
Adulescentes cnim erant in iuventute Romana ₅
quibus, more regio vivere adsuetis, displicebat respublica.  'Rex' inquiunt, 'homo est, apud quem
locus est gratiae et beneficio: leges surdae sunt et
inexorabiles, salubriorcs melioresque inopi quam
potenti.  Facillimum est hominibus errare, pericu- ₁₀
losum sine regis praesidio vivere.'  Superveniunt
legati ab regibus sine mentione reditūs bona *tantum*
repetentes.  Quorum verbis auditis aliquot dies de
hac re deliberant patres.  Interim legati alia moli-
untur: aperte bona repetentes clam consilia struunt ₁₅
quibus Tarquinii regnum recipiant.  Tum nobilium
adulescentium animos pertemptant, et eis a quibus
verba eorum placide accepta sunt litteras ab Tarquiniis reddunt: suadent ut clam noctu in urbem
reges accipiant.  Postea, ubi senatui placuit ut ₂₀
bona redderentur et necesse fuit legatis in urbe
morari ut vehicula compararent quibus regum bona

asportarent, multas horas cum coniuratis consump-
serunt: tandem eis persuaserunt ut litterae sibi ad
25 Tarquinios darentur. Datae sunt litterae ut pignus
fidei essent, sed per eas manifestum factum est
facinus. Coniurati enim, inter quos erant duo filii
Bruti consulis, ab avunculis, fratribus uxoris eius,
in societatem adsumpti, legatos, qui proximo die
30 ad Tarquinios profecturi erant, ad cenam invita-
verunt multumque cum eis de novo consilio con-
locuti sunt. Sermo autem eorum exceptus est ab
uno ex servis, qui iam antea id agi senserat sed
litterarum occasionem exspectabat. Quas ubi
35 datas esse sensit, rem ad consules detulit. Illi,
ut legatos coniuratosque deprehenderent domo
profecti, sine tumultu rem totam oppresserunt.
Proditores extemplo in vincla coniecti sunt: de
legatis autem poenae non sumptae sunt, quia ius
40 gentium valuit. Bona regis, quae ut redderentur
antea decreverant patres, propter iram regibus
reddi iam vetuerunt: a plebe diripi iusserunt.

**13** The punishment of the sons of Brutus, and the death of
the latter in a war with the Etruscans stirred up by
Tarquinius Superbus. Death of Arruns Tarquinius.

Direptis bonis regum condemnati sunt proditores,
sumptumque supplicium insigne quod necesse erat
patri poenas de liberis suis sumere. Stabant deli-
gati ad palum nobilissimi iuvenes; ceteros autem
5 nemo spectabat: omnes in consulis liberos oculos
defixos habebant consulemque miserabantur. '*Hoc
potissimum anno*' inquiunt, 'consulis filii in animum

induxerunt ut patriam liberatam, patrem libera-
torem, consulatum ex domo Iuniā ortum superbo
quondam regi, nunc infesto exsuli, prodant.' Con- 10
sules, cum in sedem suam processissent, lictores
miserunt qui poenas de adulescentibus sumerent.
Nudatos virgis caedunt securique feriunt; interea
spectabant omnes patrem voltumque eius: emine-
bat enim animus paternus *inter* publicae poenae 15
ministerium. His sicut acta erant nuntiatis, incensus Tarquinius non dolore solum, quia tanta
spes ad inritum ceciderat, sed etiam odio irāque,
cum dolo viam obsaeptam esse vidisset, circumibat
supplex Etruriae urbes, orabat maxime Veientes 20
Tarquiniensesque ne *se* extorrem, egentem, cum
liberis adulescentibus ante oculos *suos* perire sinerent. Patriam se regnumque suum repetere et
ingratos cives persequi velle. *Ferrent* opem,
*adiuvarent*. His verbis moti sunt et Veientes et 25
Tarquinienses; itaque duo duarum civitatium exercitus secuti sunt Tarquinium, ut regnum ei
repeterent belloque Romanos persequerentur. Consules obviam hostibus ierunt: Valerius quadrato
agmine pedites duxit, Brutus exploratum ante- 30
cessit. Hostium equitibus praeerat Arruns Tarquinius, filius regis: rex ipse cum legionibus
sequebatur. Arruns, Bruto agnito, inflammatus
irā, 'Ille est vir,' inquit, 'qui nos extorres expulit
e patriā. Ipse en ille nostris insignibus decoratus 35
magnifice incedit. Di regum ultores adeste.' Con-
citavit calcaribus equum atque in ipsum consulem
infestus derexit. Sensit Brutus Arruntem in se ire

et avide se certamini obtulit. Infestis armis con-
40 currerunt, neuter salutis suae memor. Itaque,
contrario ictu per parmam uterque transfixus,
moribundi ex equis lapsi sunt.

Veientes fusi fugatique sunt, Tarquinienses ab
acie *pro victis* abierunt; cum enim inluxisset nec
45 quisquam hostium in conspectu esset, P. Valerius
consul spolia legit triumphansque inde Romam
rediit. Collegae funus magno apparatu fecit, sed
multo maius decus mortuo fuit publica maestitia,
insignis quod matronae totum annum ut parentem
50 eum luxerunt.

**14** The consul, P. Valerius, takes measures to clear himself
from unfair accusations brought against him.

Tam mutabiles sunt volgi animi ut consul qui
pugnae superfuerat, P. Valerius, in invidiam sus-
picionemque mox adductus sit. Regnum eum
adfectare et credebant et dicebant homines: colle-
5 gam enim nondum subrogasse in locum Bruti et
domum in summa Velia aedificare coepisse: ibi in
alto atque munito loco arcem inexpugnabilem
futuram esse. Quae cum consulis animum ange-
rent, vocato ad concilium populo submissis fasci-
10 bus *in contionem escendit*. Gratum multitudini fuit
hoc spectaculum; insignibus enim imperii submissis maior esse videbatur populi quam consulis
maiestas. Civibus audire iussis laudabat consul
collegae sui fortunam: liberatā patriā, summo
15 honore pro republicā eum dimicasse, maturā
gloriā mortem obisse. Se autem, gloriae suae

superstitem, *ad* crimen atque invidiam superesse.
'Nunquamne ergo' inquit, 'ulla virtus adeo spec-
tata vobis erit ut suspicione violari non possit?
Eratne tam parva fiducia vestra mei ut oporteret 20
me credere me a civibus meis timeri posse? Sed
non obstabunt Publii Valerii aedes libertati vestrae,
Quirites; tuta erit vobis Velia. Non modo in
planum deferam aedes, sed etiam colli subiciam
ut vos supra suspectum me civem habitetis.' De- 25
lata est confestim materia omnis infra Veliam et
domus in imo clivo aedificata. Deinde leges novae
ab eo latae non solum regni suspicione consulem
absolverunt sed etiam tam popularem fecerunt ut
cognomen Publicolae ei datum sit. Quas leges cum 30
solus pertulisset eo consilio ut favorem inde sibi
ipse conciliaret, comitiis habitis collegam subro-
gavit. Creatus est Spurius Lucretius consul, homo
exactae aetatis, qui munera magistratūs vix obire
poterat et tam invalidus fuit ut intra paucos dies 35
mortuus sit. Suffectus est in Lucretii locum M.
Horatius Pulvillus. Haec post exactos reges domi
militiaeque gesta sunt primo anno.

The Tarquins seek the help of the king of Clusium, where- **15**
upon the senate take measures at Rome to win the support
of the plebeians. Finally Horatius Cocles saves the city.

Tarquinii, cum ad Lartem Porsinnam perfu-
gissent, orabant ne se, ex Etruscis ortos, eiusdem
sanguinis nominisque, egentes exsulare pateretur.
Is igitur Romam infesto exercitu venit. Nunquam
*alias* antea tantus terror senatum invaserat: time- 5

bant enim non solum hostes sed etiam suos cives,
ne Romana plebs metu perculsa receptis in urbem
regibus cum servitute pacem acciperet. Multa
igitur per id tempus ab senatu facta sunt ut plebis
10 animos lenirent. Annonae in primis habita est cura,
et *alii alio missi sunt* ut frumentum compararent.
Edixerunt quoque, quia sal pretio nimis magno
vēnibat, ne privatis diutius liceret eum vendere,
portoriisque et tributo plebem liberaverunt ut
15 divites conferrent: eos enim tantum pecuniae
habere ut onus facile ferre possent. Quae indulgentia patrum adeo concordem civitatem tenuit ut
nemo malis artibus postea tam popularis esset
quam tum bene imperando senatus fuit.

20     Cum hostes adessent, Romani in urbem ex agris
demigrant, urbem ipsam praesidiis saepiunt. Aliae
partes muris, aliae Tiberi obiecto tutae esse vide-
bantur; et quamquam per pontem sublicium iter
hostibus paene datum est, urbem servavit Hora-
25 tius Cocles, qui forte in statione pontis erat positus.
Cum enim Ianiculum repentino impetu captum
esse atque hostes inde citatos decurrere trepidam-
que suorum turbam arma ordinesque relinquere
vidisset, singulos reprehendebat obsistens obtes-
30 tansque. 'Nequiquam' inquit, 'deserto *praesidio*
fugitis: nam si pontem transieritis et a tergo reli-
queritis, mox plus hostium in Palatio Capitolioque
erit quam in Ianiculo. Itaque moneo ut pontem
ferro, igni, quācumque vi poteritis, interrumpatis.
35 Hostium impetum corpore meo solus excipiam.'
Vasit inde in primum aditum pontis et ipso mira-

culo audaciae obstupefecit hostes. Duos tamen
cum eo pudor tenuit, Sp. Larcium ac T. Hermi-
nium, ambos genere factisque claros. Cum his
primam periculi procellam parumper sustinuit. 40
Deinde eos quoque ipsos, exiguā parte pontis
relictā, cedere in tutum coegit. Hostes, sublato
clamore, undique in unum hostem tela coniciebant.
Quae cum in obiecto scuto cuncta haesissent, et ille
ingenti gradu pontem nihilominus obtineret, iam 45
impetu conabantur virum detrudere cum auditus
est simul fragor rupti pontis, simul clamor ab
Romanis ob gaudium perfecti operis sublatus. Tum
Cocles, magnā voce precatus ut secundo flumine se
acciperet, in Tiberim armatus desiluit, et incolumis 50
ad suos tranavit.

### C. Mucius' unsuccessful attempt to kill Porsinna. 16

Porsinna, primo conatu repulsus, urbem obsidere
constituit, praesidioque in Ianiculo locato ipse in
plano ripisque Tiberis castra posuit; brevique adeo
infestum omnem Romanum agrum *reddidit* ut non
cetera solum ex agris sed pecus quoque omne in 5
urbem compelleretur, neque quisquam extra portas
pecus propellere auderet. Tandem vero, insidiis a
Valerio consule paratis, finis factus est Etruscis
tam effuse vagandi. Obsidio erat nihilominus et
frumenti cum summā caritate inopia, sedendoque 10
expugnaturum se urbem sperabat Porsinna. Tum
C. Mucius, adulescens nobilis, primo ignaris omnibus in hostium castra penetrare constituit; deinde,
veritus ne a custodibus Romanis deprehensus re-

¹⁵ traheretur et *pro transfugā haberetur*, senatum
adiit. 'Transire Tiberim' inquit, 'patres, et hostium castra, si potero, intrare volo. Magnum, dis
adiuvantibus, in animo est facinus.' Rem adpro-
bant patres. Mucius, abdito intra vestem ferro,
20 proficiscitur. Cum ad castra hostium venisset, in
confertissimā turbā prope regium tribunal con-
stitit. Ibi cum stipendium militibus forte daretur
et scriba cum rege sedens pari fere ornatu multa
ageret eumque milites adirent, veritus sciscitari
25 uter Porsinna esset, ne rege ignorato quis ipse
esset aperiret, scribam pro rege obtruncavit. Cum
vero, concursu ad clamorem facto, comprehensus
et a regiis satellitibus retractus esset, ante tribunal
regis destitutus, 'Romanus' inquit, 'civis sum, C.
30 Mucium me vocant. Hostis hostem occīdere volui.
Nec unus in te hos animos gessi; longus post me
ordo est idem decus petentium. Huiusmodi bellum
tibi iuvenes Romani indicimus: noli aciem, noli
proelium timere: uni tibi et cum *singulis* res erit.'
35 Tum rex, irā infensus periculoque perterritus,
'Ignes tibi' inquit, 'circumdari iubebo, nisi statim
dixeris quas insidiarum minas istis verbis mihi
iacias.' Extemplo Mucius, 'En tibi,' inquit, 'ut
sentias quam vile sit corpus eis qui magnam
40 gloriam vident,' dextramque accenso ad sacrificium
igni iniecit. Quam cum torreri videret Porsinna,
admiratus quam fortis esset Mucius, 'Tu vero abī,'
inquit, 'intactum te inviolatumque hinc dimitto.'
Tum Mucius 'Quoniam' inquit, 'est apud te virtuti
45 honor, hanc rem tibi aperiam: trecenti principes

iuventutis Romanae nos te hac ratione adgressuros
coniuravimus. Mea prima sors fuit: ceteri suo
quisque tempore aderunt. Tu vero, qui nescis
quando quisque adfuturus sit, in periculo semper
versaberis.' Mucium dimissum, cui postea Scaevo- 50
lae a clade dextrae manūs cognomen datum est,
legati a Porsinna Romam secuti ut Tarquinii in
regnum restituerentur nequiquam monebant. Romani autem, ut Porsinna a Ianiculo praesidium
deduceret, coacti sunt obsides dare. Patres C. 55
Mucium propter virtutem agro trans Tiberim sito
donaverunt.

Cloelia.                                            **17**

Ergo ita honoratā virtute feminae quoque ad
publica decora sunt excitatae. Et Cloelia virgo,
una ex obsidibus, cum castra Etruscorum forte
haud procul a ripā Tiberis locata essent, frustrata
custodes, dux agminis virginum inter tela hostium 5
Tiberim tranavit, incolumesque omnes Romam ad
propinquos restituit. Quod ubi regi nuntiatum est,
primo irā incensus legatos Romam misit qui Cloeliam obsidem deposcerent: ceteras se haud *magni
facere.* Deinde in admirationem versus 'Supra 10
Coclites Muciosque' inquit, 'est hoc facinus:
quamquam igitur, nisi dedita erit obses, pro rupto
foedus habebo, si dedita erit, intactam inviola-
tamque ad *suos* eam remittam. Interrogate igitur,
legati, num Cloeliam obsidem dedere parati sint 15
Romani.' Utrique fidem praestiterunt: et Romani
pignus pacis ex foedere restituerunt et apud regem

Etruscorum non tuta solum sed etiam honorata
fuit virtus, laudatamque virginem parte obsidum
20 se donaturum dixit; ipsa *quos vellet* eligeret. Pro-
ductis omnibus impubes elegisse dicitur. Pace
redintegratā Romani novam in femina virtutem
novo genere honoris, statuā equestri, donaverunt:
in summā Sacrā viā posita est virgo equo insidens.

**18** Tarquinius Superbus, dismissed by Porsinna, goes into
exile. Death of P. Valerius Publicola. Appointment of a
dictator for the first time.

Mox autem legati a Porsinna Romam missi a
senatu petierunt ut Tarquinii in regnum reduce-
rentur. Quibus cum responsum esset senatum ad
regem legatos missurum, missus est confestim
5 *honoratissimus quisque* ex patribus, ut in perpetuum
mentio eius rei finiretur. Qui cum ad Porsinnam
venissent, dixerunt Romanos in animum induxisse
ut hostibus potius quam regibus portas pateface-
rent. 'Proinde' inquiunt, 'si salvam esse vis Romam,
10 oramus ut liberam eam esse patiaris: qui enim
libertati erit in urbe nostrā finis, īdem urbi quoque
erit.' Rex, verecundiā victus, 'Quoniam id certum
vobis atque obstinatum est,' inquit, 'neque ego
obtundam saepius eadem nequiquam agendo, nec
15 Tarquinios spe auxilii, quod nullum in me est,
frustrabor: alium, sive bello opus est sive quiete,
exsilio quaerant locum.' Tum Tarquinius, spe
omni reditūs incisā, exsulatum ad generum,
Octavium Mamilium, Tusculum abiit: Romanis
20 pax fida cum Porsinnā fuit.

Paucis post annis P. Valerius, belli pacisque
artibus omnium consensu *princeps*, moritur, gloriā
insigni, copiis autem familiaribus adeo exiguis ut
funeri sumptus deesset: de publico est datus.
Luxerunt eum matronae ut Brutum.                    25

Haud multo postea, cum bellum Latinum immi-
neret, placuit ut dictator primum crearetur, neque
tamen satis constat quis primus creatus sit; tot
enim erant temporum errores, *aliter apud alios
auctores* ordinatis magistratibus ut ne de consulibus 30
quidem digerere posset Livius *qui consules secundum quos fuissent* nec quid quōque anno actum
esset. Postquam vero, creato dictatore, praeferri
secures viderunt, tantus metus plebem incessit ut
intentiores essent ad dicto parendum.               35

War with the Latins, and the battle of Lake Regillus.    **19**

Nec ultra dilatum est Latinum bellum, iam per
aliquot annos gliscens. Aulus Postumius dictator
et Titus Aebutius magister equitum, magnis
copiis peditum equitumque ad lacum Regillum
profecti, in agro Tusculano agmini hostium occur- 5
rerunt: et quia Tarquinios esse in exercitu Latinorum audierunt, extemplo conflixerunt. Ergo
etiam proelium aliquanto gravius atque atrocius
fuit quam cetera. Duces enim non solum consilio
rem rexerunt, sed etiam suis ipsi corporibus dimi- 10
caverunt. In Postumium primā in acie suos
adhortantem instruentemque Tarquinius Superbus,
quamquam iam aetate et viribus erat gravior,
equum infestus derexit, volneratusque concursu

15 suorum in tutum receptus est. Et ad alterum
cornu Aebutius magister equitum in Octavium
Mamilium impetum fecit, tantaque vis infestis
hastis venientium fuit ut brachium Aebutii traiec-
tum sit, Mamilii pectus percussum. Hunc quidem
20 in secundam aciem Latini receperunt: Aebutius,
quod saucio brachio telum tenere non poterat, ex
pugnā excessit. Latinus dux, volnere nullo modo
deterritus, proelium ciebat, et quia suos perculsos
videbat, arcessivit cohortem exsulum Romanorum,
25 cui Lucii Tarquinii filius praeerat. Ea, quia erepta
bona reciperandi causā summā irā pugnabat, pugnam parumper restituit.

Referentibus iam pedem ab eā parte Romanis
dictator Postumius, postquam exsules ferociter
30 citato agmine invehi, suos perculsos cedere ani-
madvertit, cohorti suae, quam praesidii causā
circa se habebat, dedit signum ut quem suorum
fugientem *vidissent* pro hoste haberent. Ita propter
metum ancipitem versi sunt a fugā in hostem
35 Romani, et restituta est acies. Cohors dictatoris
tum primum proelium iniit. Integris corporibus
animisque fessos adorti exsules caedunt. Tum
imperator Latinus, cum cohortem exsulum a dictatore Romano paene circumventam vidisset, ex
40 subsidiariis manipulos aliquot in primam aciem
secum rapuit. Hos agmine venientes T. Herminius
legatus conspicatus interque eos insignem veste
armisque Mamilium agnoscens, tantā vi cum hostium duce proelium iniit ut et uno ictu transfixum
45 per latus occīderit Mamilium, et ipse telo percussus,

cum victor in castra esset relatus, inter primam
curationem exspiraverit. Tum ad equites dictator
advolat, obtestans ut, fesso iam pedite, descendant
ex equis et partem pugnae capiant. Dicto parue-
runt: desiliunt ex equis, provolant in primum, par- 50
mas hostibus obiciunt. Recipit extemplo animum
pedestris acies. Tum demum impulsi sunt Latini
perculsaque acies inclinavit. Equitibus admoti
sunt equi ut hostem persequi possent: secuta est
et pedestris acies; ibi nihil aut divinae aut humanae 55
opis dictator praetermittens aedem *Castori* vovisse
fertur ac militibus praemia pronuntiasse. Tantus-
que ardor fuit ut eodem impetu, quo fuderant
hostem, Romani castra ceperint. Hoc modo ad
lacum Regillum *pugnatum est.*                          60

War with the Volscians, Auruncans, Aequians and Sabines. **20**
The first 'strike' of the plebeians, in consequence of which
they secured magistrates of their own, called 'plebeian
tribunes,' to safeguard their rights (494 B.C.).

Paucis post annis, consulibus Appio Claudio et
Publio Servilio, mors Tarquinii nuntiata est:
mortuus erat Cumis, quo post fractas Latinorum
opes ad Aristodemum tyrannum se contulerat.

Mox bellum Volscum imminebat: simul civitas 5
intestino inter patres plebemque odio flagrabat,
maxime propter eos qui ob aes alienum in vincla
coniecti erant. Consules autem, ut seditionem com-
primerent, statim intervenerunt. Inter haec maior
alius terror: equites Latinorum, qui iam cum 10
Romanis amicitiam inierant, cum tumultuoso

nuntio advolant, Volscos infesto exercitu ut urbem oppugnarent venire. Primo plebs se *nomina daturos esse* negaverunt: patres militarent, patres 15 arma caperent, ut penes eosdem essent et pericula et praemia belli. Cum vero consul edixisset ne quis civem Romanum nomen dare prohiberet, extemplo undique ex tota urbe se proripiebant homines *ex privato* in forum ut nomina darent. 20 Consul copias contra hostem eduxit: mox autem, hostibus fusis atque fugatis castrisque eorum captis direptisque, victorem exercitum cum max- imā gloriā suā reduxit.

Mox legati Auruncorum senatum adeunt: 'Nisi 25 a Volsco agro' inquiunt, 'extemplo decesseritis, nos bellum vobis inferemus.' Cum legatis simul exercitus Auruncorum domo profectus erat. Cuius fama Romanos tanto tumultu concivit ut statim cum Auruncis signa contulerint proelioque uno 30 debellaverint.

Proximo anno Aequi Latinum agrum invaserunt: quo facto legati Latinorum ab senatu petebant ut aut mitterent subsidium aut se ipsos agros tuendi causa arma capere sinerent. Tutius visum est 35 Latinos inermes defendere quam arma retractare pati. T. Veturius, alter consulum, in Aequos missus est: is finis populationibus fuit. Cesserunt enim a campis Aequi et summis montium iugis se tutabantur. Alter consul, A. Verginius, in Volscos 40 profectus, victoriam insignem de eis reportavit. Interim dictator, M'. Valerius, Sabinos fudit fuga- vitque castrisque exuit.

Ita tribus bellis re bene gestā, tamen de domesti-
carum rerum eventu et patres et plebs solliciti
erant. Dictator enim, cum pro victore populo ad 45
senatum frustra rettulisset quid de aere alieno fieri
placeret, dictaturā se abdicavit. Timor inde patres
incessit: 'Si dimissus erit exercitus,' inquiunt,
'rursus coniurationes erunt.' Itaque per causam
renovati ab Aequis belli educi ex urbe legiones 50
iusserunt. Quo facto maturata est seditio: plebs
in Sacrum montem secessit. Ibi sine ullo duce,
vallo fossaque communitis castris, quieti per
aliquot dies manebant, neque lacessiti neque
lacessentes. In urbe pavor ingens erat, et patribus 55
placuit Menenium Agrippam legatum ad plebem
mittere. Is 'Membra estis reipublicae Romanae,'
inquit, 'et patres et plebs, sicut manūs et ōs et
dentes membra sunt corporis mei. Nolite igitur
bellum inter vos gerere. Nisi enim auxilium alius 60
alii feretis, omnes interibitis.' Talibus verbis
mentes eorum adeo flexit ut in concordiam redire
constituerint. Plebi concessi sunt magistratūs
sacrosancti, quibus auxilium plebi adversus consules ferre liceret. Ita tribuni plebis creati sunt 65
duo: hi *tres collegas* sibi creaverunt.

Success of Cn. Marcius Coriolanus, followed later by his **21**
disgrace. He goes into exile and becomes one of the
Volscian commanders-in-chief.

Consulibus Sp. Cassio et Postumo Cominio cum
Latinis populis foedus ictum est. Ut id feriret
alter consulum Romae mansit; alter, ad Volscum

bellum missus, magnā vi adortus est Coriolos. Erat
5 tum in castris inter primores iuvenum Cn. Marcius,
adulescens et consilio et manu promptus, cui cognomen postea Coriolano fuit. Is forte in statione
erat, cum exercitum Romanum Coriolos obsidentem
atque in oppidanos, quos intus clausos habebat,
10 intentum Volscae legiones subito invaserunt,
eodemque tempore ex oppido eruperunt hostes.
Quorum impetum erumpentium Marcius primum
cum delectā militum manu retudit: tum per
patentem portam ferox inrupit, caedeque in
15 proximā parte urbis factā ignem temere arreptum
aedificiis muro imminentibus iniecit. Ita fusis
Volscis Coriolisque oppido capto summā laude
adfectus est Cn. Marcius.

Proximo anno Romae caritas primum annonae
20 erat, quia ob secessionem plebis agri inculti fuerant,
deinde fames extrema, interissentque servi utique
et plebs nisi consules providissent, hominibus
passim dimissis qui frumentum coemerent. Tum,
magnā vi frumenti ex Siciliā advectā, delibera-
25 verunt patres *quanti* plebi dandum esset. Marcius
Coriolanus autem, tribuniciae potestati inimicus,
'Si annonam,' inquit, 'veterem volunt, ius pristinum
patribus ab eis reddendum est. Cur plebeios magistratūs video? Egone hanc indignitatem diutius
30 patiar quam necesse est? Secedat nunc plebs:
patet via in Sacrum montem: rapiant frumenta
ex agris sicut *tertio anno* rapuerunt.' Haec sententia eius et senatui nimis atrox visa est et plebem ob iram paene armavit; in exeuntem eum e

curia impetus factus esset, nisi peropportune tri- 35
buni diem dixissent. Contemptim primo Marcius
audiebat minas tribunicias: postea vero, cum die
dictā non adesset, condemnatus est absens et in
Volscos exsulatum abiit, minitans patriae et iam
tum hostilem animum gerens. Venientem eum 40
Volsci benigne exceperunt, benigniusque in dies
colebant: hospitio eum accepit Attius Tullius, qui
longe princeps Volscorum tum erat Romanisque
semper infestus. Consilia contulerunt de Romano
bello, sed haud facile credebant plebem suam im- 45
pelli posse ut totiens infeliciter temptata arma
caperent. Tandem vero *fraude et dolo* effecerunt
ut Volsci omnes bellum Romanis indicerent.

Imperatores ad id bellum ex omnium sententiā
lecti sunt Attius Tullius et Cn. Marcius, exsul 50
Romanus, in quo aliquanto plus spei est repositum.
Quam spem nequaquam fefellit, adeo ut plebs
Romana senatum pacem petere coegerit. 'Legati'
inquiunt, 'ad Volscos vobis mittendi sunt et pax
petenda.' Hi autem atrox responsum rettulerunt: 55
deinde eidem iterum missi non recepti sunt in
castra. Sacerdotes quoque suis insignibus velati
ierunt supplices ad castra hostium, sed nihilo magis
quam legati animum Marcii flexerunt.

Coriolanus is overcome by his mother's entreaties.    **22**

Tum matronae ad Veturiam, matrem Coriolani,
Volumniamque uxorem frequentes coeunt. In-
certum est utrum id publicum consilium an

muliebris timor fuerit, sed *haud dubium est quin*
5 et Veturia, magno natu mulier, et Volumnia, duos
parvos ex Marcio filios secum ferens, in castra
hostium ierint, et mulieres precibus lacrimisque
urbem defenderint quam armis viri defendere non
poterant. Ubi ad castra venerunt nuntiatumque
10 est Coriolano ingens mulierum agmen adesse, primo
multo obstinatior erat adversus lacrimas muliebres.
Deinde familiarium quidam, qui insignem maestitiā
inter ceteras agnoverat Veturiam, inter nurum
nepotesque stantem, 'Nisi me frustrantur' inquit,
15 'oculi, mater tibi coniunxque et liberi adsunt.'
Coriolanus cum paene amens consternatus ab sede
suā surrexisset et matrem amplecti vellet, mulier
in iram ex precibus versa, 'Permitte' inquit,
'priusquam amplexum tuum accepero, ut sciam
20 utrum ad hostem an ad filium venerim, utrum
captiva an mater in castris tuis sim! Num potuisti
populari hanc terram, quae te genuit atque aluit?
Nonne, cum in conspectu Roma fuit, succurrit
tibi: Intra illa moenia domus ac penates mei sunt,
25 mater, coniunx liberique? Ergo ego nisi mater
essem, Roma non oppugnaretur; nisi filium habe-
rem, libera in liberā patriā mortua essem. Sed ego
nihil iam pati possum, nec, quamquam sum miser-
rima, diu futura sum: hos respice, quos, si pergis,
30 aut immatura mors aut longa servitus manet:
patriam respice, quae, si tecum loquatur, libertatem a te vehementissime poscat.' Uxor deinde
ac liberi amplexi fletusque ab omni turbā mulierum
ortus et comploratio sui patriaeque fregerunt tan-

dem virum. Amplexus suos inde dimisit; ipse 35
retro ab urbe castra movit.

### The Fabian House. 23

Tribus insequentibus annis consules gentis
Fabiae erant: primum Quintus Fabius, qui, de-
victis Volscis Aequisque, quidquid ex hostibus
captum erat vendidit ac in publicum redegit, tum
Caeso Fabius, deinde M. Fabius, Caesonis frater. 5
Fabium inde nomen post tres continuos consulatus
summo honore est habitum. Tum iterum consules
facti sunt hi tres Fabii. Consule Marco, dum cum
Veientibus Etruscisque bellum gerunt Romani,
gens Fabia inter primores insignis fuit. Ex his 10
Quintum Fabium, inter multas hostium manūs
incautum versantem, gladio per pectus transfixit
Tuscus quidam. Sensit utraque acies unius viri
casum, cedebantque inde Romani, cum M. Fabius
consul transiluit iacentis corpus, obiectāque parmā, 15
'Num hoc iurastis,' inquit, 'milites, fugientes vos
in castra redituros? At ego iniuratus aut victor
revertar, aut prope te hic, Quinte Fabi, dimicans
cadam.' Consuli tum respondit Caeso Fabius:
'Verbisne istis, frater,' inquit, 'ut pugnent te im- 20
petraturum credis? Di impetrabunt, per quos
iuraverunt. Nos, ut decet proceres, ut Fabio
nomine est dignum, pugnando potius quam adhor-
tando militum animos accendamus.' Sic in primum
infestis hastis provolant duo Fabii, totamque aciem 25
secum moverunt.

Proelio ab unā parte restituto nihilo segnius in

cornu altero Cn. Manlius consul pugnam ciebat.
Cum vero gravi volnere ictus ex acie cessisset,
30 milites eum interfectum esse rati gradum rettulerunt, cessissentque loco nisi consul alter cum aliquot
turmis equitum in eam partem citato equo advectus
rem inclinatam sustinuisset. Manlius quoque re-
stituendae aciei causā se ipse coram offert. Duorum
35 consulum cognita ora accendunt militum animos.
Simul hostes, multitudine freti, subtracta sub-
sidia mittunt ad castra oppugnanda. In quae
haud magno certamine impetu facto, cum praedae
magis quam pugnae memores tempus tererent,
40 *triarii* Romani, qui primam inruptionem sustinere
non potuerant, missis ad consules nuntiis quo loco
res esset, conglobati ad praetorium redeunt, et suā
sponte ipsi proelium renovant. Et Manlius consul
in castra revectus militibus ad omnes portas
45 oppositis hostibus viam clauserat. Mox autem
mortifero volnere ictus cecidit, fusique sunt omnes
qui circa erant. Tuscis crescit audacia, Romanos
terror per tota castra trepidos agit, et ad extremum res venisset, ni *legati*, rapto consulis corpore,
50 unā portā viam hostibus patefecissent. Eā erum-
punt, consternatoque agmine abeuntes in victorem
alterum consulem incidunt. Ibi iterum caesi
fusique sunt passim.

**24** The famous exploit of the Fabii.

Proximo anno in Veienti bello clades accepta est
propter temeritatem alterius consulis, actumque
esset de exercitu, nisi alter consul, Caeso Fabius,

in tempore *subsidio* venisset. Postea gens **Fabia**
senatum adiit. Consul pro gente loquitur: 'Vos,' 5
inquit, 'patres conscripti, alia bella curate, Fabios
hostes Veientibus date. Pollicemur tutam ibi
maiestatem Romani nominis fore. Nostrum id
nobis velut familiare bellum privato sumptu
gerere in animo est: neve milites illic neve pecu- 10
niam suppeditet respublica.' Gratiae ingentes
actae sunt. Consul e curiā egressus comitante
Fabiorum agmine, qui in vestibulo curiae senatūs
consultum exspectantes constiterant, domum rediit. Iussi sunt armati postero die ad limen con- 15
sulis adesse; domos inde discesserunt.

Mānat totā urbe rumor, Fabios ad caelum laudi-
bus ferunt: familiam unam subisse civitatis onus.
Fabii postero die arma capiunt, quo iussi erant
conveniunt. Consul paludatus egrediens in vesti- 20
bulo gentem omnem suam agmine instructam videt:
acceptus in medium signa ferri iubet. Nunquam
exercitus aut minor numero aut clarior famā et
admiratione hominum per urbem incessit: **VI** et
**CCC** milites, omnes patricii, omnes unius gentis, 25
quorum nemo dux spernendus erat, ibant, unius
familiae viribus Veienti populo pestem minitantes.
Sequebatur turba, partim propria cognatorum
sodaliumque, partim publica, favore et admiratione
stupens. Ire fortes, ire felices iubent, et inceptis 30
eventūs pares reddere. Tum, praetereuntibus
Fabiis Capitolium arcemque et alia templa, deos
precantur ut illud agmen faustum atque felix
mittant, sospites brevi in patriam ad parentes

35 restituant. Inritae autem fuerunt hae preces. In-
felici viā dextro *Iano* portae Carmentalis profecti
ad Cremeram flumen perveniunt. Is opportunus
visus est locus communiendo praesidio, ibique gens
una populi Romani saepe de opulentissimā, ut tum
40 res erant, Etruscā civitate victoriam reportavit.
Mox Veientes consilium capiunt hostes insidiis
captandi. Itaque et pecora praedantibus aliquotiens, velut si casu incidissent, obviam acta sunt,
et agrestium fugā vasti relicti sunt agri, et sub-
45 sidia armatorum ad arcendas populationes missa
saepius simulato quam vero pavore refugerunt.
Iamque Fabii adeo contempserant hostem ut sua
invicta arma neque loco neque tempore ullo susti-
neri posse crederent. Hac spe provecti ad con-
50 specta procul a Cremerā, magno campo interia-
cente, pecora decurrerunt. Et cum improvidi
effuso cursu insidias circa ipsum iter locatas *superassent*, palatique passim raperent pecora, subito ex
insidiis consurgunt hostes. Primo clamor circum-
55 latus Fabios exterruit, deinde tela ab omni parte
incidebant; coeuntibusque Etruscis iam continenti
agmine armatorum saepti sunt. Tum in unum locum
se omnes inclinant. Eo nīsi corporibus armisque
ruperunt viam. Duxit via in leniter editum collem.
60 Inde primo restiterunt; mox pepulerunt etiam
subeuntes: auxilioque loci vicissent, nisi Veientes
iugo circummissi in verticem collis evasissent. Ita
superior rursus hostis factus est. Fabii caesi sunt
ad unum omnes, praesidiumque expugnatum. Tre-
65 centos sex perisse satis convenit.

# NOTES

## 2

**5. forte**, adverb, 'as it happened.'

**19. aliquantum spatii.** *Spatii* is an 'integral' genitive; it denotes the whole from which a part, here *aliquantum*, is taken.

**20. cum...vidit.** In this clause of time, which *follows* the main clause, *cum* means 'when suddenly.'

## 3

**8. Re vera**, 'in reality,' 'as a matter of fact.'

**14. secutus.** A few deponent *perf.* participles, *e.g. secutus* in this passage, have *present* meaning.

## 4

**7. rata** is equivalent in meaning to a present participle.

**11. ex.** Here translate by 'from.'

**22. se...ipso.** At *se* there begins Tarquinius' speech, which is given in the form of dependent statements. It ends at *ipso*.

**25. in.** Here translate by 'towards.'

**26. certasse.** *Certare* is used here in the meaning 'to vie with.'

## 5

**5. fastigio**, 'by means of a slope,' trans. 'down a slope.'

**8. Servio Tullio.** By the Latin idiom the dative, which is used by attraction to the case of the pronoun *cui*, is preferred to the nominative in expressions of this kind.

**20. habere ut** = to treat as.

## 6

**23.** From **sopitum esse regem** to **exsecuturum** Tanaquil's speech is given in dependent statements.

## 7

**19. infestior.** *Infestus* is here used in the sense of 'open to attack,' 'endangered.'

**34. servum...datum.** Dependent statements, suggested by 'orationem habuit.'

**39. me vivo,** 'in my lifetime.' Abl. absolute with verb unexpressed owing to the want of a pres. participle of *sum*.

## 8

**12. cum...indictus est.** Cf. note on *cum...vidit* in chap. 2.

**35. saluti fuit.** *Saluti* may be translated as a nominative in English. It forms the predicate with *fuit* and is called a 'Predicative Dative.'

## 9

**20. Bruti.** The adjective *brutus* has the meaning 'stupid.'
**36. alio.** Here an adverb, meaning 'in another direction.'

## 10

*Genealogical table to illustrate the relationships*
*of the Tarquins*

Demaratus

```
                        Demaratus
            ┌───────────────┴───────────────┐
   L. Tarquinius Priscus              Arruns Tarquinius
      ┌────────┼──────────┬──────────┐        │
L. Tarquinius   Arruns  Tarquinia   Egerius
 Superbus
  ┌──────┼───────┐        │              │
Titus  Arruns  Sextus  L. Iunius     Tarquinius
                        Brutus        Collatinus
```

**12. cum singulis amicis,** 'with one friend each.'
**39. duce Bruto.** Cf. *me vivo* in chap. 7.
**45. Romanos homines...factos.** See note to chap. 6.

## 12

**12. tantum** here, as often, means 'only.'

## 13

**7. Hoc potissimum anno,** 'In this year above all others'; *potissimum* means 'preferably.'

**15. inter,** 'during the fulfilment of.'

**21. se...suos.** *Se* here refers to the main subject in a clause reflecting Tarquinius' will (indirect reflexive use); *suos* refers to the subject of *sinerent* (the regular use of the direct reflexive).

**24. Ferrent...adiuvarent.** Subjunctives of 'desire' (without *ut* because they occur in *continuous* reported speech), representing imperatives of the actual speech.

**44. pro victis,** 'as good as defeated,' 'virtually defeated.'

## 14

**10. in contionem escendit,** 'he mounted (a platform) to address the assembly.'

**17. ad,** 'to face.'

## 15

**5. alias,** adverb, 'at any other time.'

**11. alii alio missi sunt,** 'men were sent in different directions.'

**30. praesidio.** Here = 'post.'

## 16

**4. reddidit** (infestum). Here = 'rendered, made.'

**15. pro transfuga haberetur,** 'be regarded as a deserter.'

**34. singulis.** Cf. note on *cum singulis amicis* in chap. 10.

## 17

**9. magni facere.** *Magni* is a 'Genitive of Value': with *facere* the meaning is 'rate at a high price,' and therefore 'care much about.'

**14. suos.** The adjective *suus* is sometimes used to refer to some word other than the subject of the sentence, etc.; here to the object *eam.*

**20. quos vellet.** The subjunctive is used because the clause is itself subordinated to a subjunctive that denotes 'desire,' *eligeret.* For *eligeret* cf. the note on *ferrent...adiuvarent* in chap. 13.

## 18

**5. honoratissimus quisque,** 'all the most distinguished.'

**22. princeps.** Here used in the sense of 'first.'

**29. aliter apud alios auctores,** 'differently in different authors.'

**31. qui consules secundum quos fuissent.** Double interrogative in the one clause.

## 19

**33. vidissent.** For the mood in the relative clause cf. the note on *quos vellet* in chap. 17.

**56. Castori.** *Castor* is here used for Castor and Pollux, the twin brothers otherwise called, by their Greek name, the Dioscuri. According to Cicero 'ex equis pugnare visi sunt' at the battle of Lake Regillus.

**60. pugnatum est.** The impersonal use of the passive, often used in Latin when the doers of an action are not named: 'fighting took place.'

## 20

**13. nomina daturos esse.** *Nomen dare* = 'to enlist, to volunteer.'

**19. ex privato,** 'from the places where they were confined.'

**66. tres collegas.** The number of the plebeian tribunes was afterwards increased from 5 to 10.

## 21

**25. quanti.** A 'Genitive of Price.'

**32. tertio anno** = tertio antehac anno 'two years ago.'

**47. fraude et dolo.** This trick took the form of frightening the senate into expelling from Rome a number of Volscians, who had come there to attend some games, which were to be celebrated anew with special magnificence by way of expiation of a technical offence against Jupiter (Livy ii. 36 ff.).

## 22

**4. haud dubium est quin,** 'there is no doubt that.'

## 23

**40. triarii.** Here used of the reserve left to guard the camp.

**49. legati.** Here = 'officers.'

## 24

**4. subsidio.** Dative, 'as a help,' 'to its help.'

**36. Iano.** Here translate 'arch.'

**52. superassent.** Trans. 'had got safely past.'

# PASSAGES FROM OVID'S *FASTI*

## TO ILLUSTRATE CERTAIN STORIES IN THIS BOOK

### I. *To illustrate chapter* 1

Est locus, antiqui Capreae dixere paludem:
　　forte tuis illic, Romule, iura dabas.
sol fugit, et removent subeuntia nubila caelum,
　　et gravis effusis decidit imber aquis.
hinc tonat, hinc missis abrumpitur ignibus aether.
　　fit fuga, rex patriis astra petebat equis.
luctus erat, falsaeque patres in crimine caedis:
　　haesissetque animis forsitan illa fides:
sed Proculus Longā veniebat Iulius Albā,
　　lunaque fulgebat, nec facis usus erat,
cum subito motu saepes tremuere sinistrae:
　　rettulit ille gradus, horrueruntque comae:
pulcher et humano maior trabeāque decorus
　　Romulus in mediā visus adesse viā
et dixisse simul 'prohibe lugere Quirites,
　　nec violent lacrimis numina nostra suis.
tura ferant plācentque novum pia turba Quirinum
　　et patrias artes militiamque colant.'
iussit et in tenues oculis evanuit auras.
　　convocat hic populos iussaque verba refert.

(II. 491–510.)

## II. *To illustrate chapter* 7

Tullia coniugio, sceleris mercede, peracto
   his solita est dictis exstimulare virum:
'quid iuvat esse pares, te nostrae caede sororis,
   meque tui fratris, si pia vita placet?
vivere debuerant et vir meus et tua coniunx,
   si nullum ausuri maius eramus opus.
et caput et regnum facio dotale parentis.
   si vir es, i, dictas exige dotis opes!
regia res scelus est! socero cape regna necato,
   et nostras patrio sanguine tinge manus!'
talibus instinctus solio privatus in alto
   sederat. attonitum volgus ad arma ruit:
hinc cruor, hinc caedes, infirmaque vincitur aetas:
   sceptra gener socero rapta Superbus habet.

(VI. 587–600.)

## III. *To illustrate chapter* 9

Ecce, nefas visu, mediis altaribus anguis
   exit et exstinctis ignibus exta rapit.
consulitur Phoebus. sors est ita reddita: 'matri
   qui dederit princeps oscula victor erit.'
oscula quisque suae matri properata tulerunt,
   non intellecto credula turba deo.
Brutus erat stulti sapiens imitator, ut esset
   tutus ab insidiis, dire Superbe, tuis.
ille iacens pronus matri dedit oscula Terrae,
   creditus offenso procubuisse pede.

(II. 711–720.)

### IV.  *To illustrate chapter* 10

Ultima Tarquinius Romanae gentis habebat
  regna, vir iniustus, fortis ad arma tamen.
ceperat hic alias, alias everterat urbes,
  et Gabios turpi fecerat arte suos.

Brutus clamore Quirites
  concitat et regis facta nefanda refert.
Tarquinius cum prole fugit: capit annua consul
  iura: dies regnis illa suprema fuit.

(II. 687–690, and 849–852.)

### V.  *To illustrate chapter* 24

Una domus vires et onus susceperat urbis:
  sumunt gentiles arma professa manus:
egreditur castris miles generosus ab isdem,
  e *quis* dux fieri quilibet aptus erat.
Carmentis portae dextra est via proxima Iano:
  ire per hanc noli, quisquis es; omen habet.
ut celeri passu Cremeram tetigēre rapacem,
  (turbidus hibernis ille fluebat aquis)
castra loco ponunt.  destrictis ensibus ipsi
  Tyrrhenum valido Marte per agmen eunt;
non aliter quam cum Libycā de rupe leones
  invadunt sparsos lata per arva greges.
diffugiunt hostes inhonestaque volnera tergo
  accipiunt: Tusco sanguine terra rubet.
sic iterum, sic saepe cadunt.  ubi vincere aperte
  non datur, insidias armaque tecta parant.

l. 4.  quis here = *quibus.*

campus erat; campi claudebant ultima colles
  silvaque montanas occulere apta feras.
in medio paucos armentaque rara relinquunt,
  cetera virgultis abdita turba latet.
ecce velut torrens undis pluvialibus auctus
  aut nive, quae Zephyro victa tepente fluit,
per sata perque vias fertur nec, ut ante solebat,
  riparum clausas margine finit aquas:
sic Fabii vallem latis discursibus implent,
  quodque vident, sternunt: nec metus alter inest.
quo ruitis, generosa domus? male creditis hosti:
  simplex nobilitas, perfida tela cave!
fraude perit virtus. in apertos undique campos
  prosiliunt hostes et latus omne tenent.
quid faciant pauci contra tot milia fortes?
  quidve, quod in misero tempore restet, adest?
sicut aper longe silvis Laurentibus actus
  fulmineo celeres dissipat ore canes,
mox tamen ipse perit, sic non moriuntur inulti
  volneraque alternā dantque feruntque manu.
una dies Fabios ad bellum miserat omnes:
  ad bellum missos perdidit una dies.

(II. 197–236.)

# MAIN CONSTRUCTIONS DEALT WITH
## IN THE *B* EXERCISES

I. Deponent perfect participle.

II. Ablative Absolute.

III. Dependent statement (present and future infinitives).

IV. Dependent statement (perfect infinitive).
Verbs like *iubeo*, which take present infinitive only.

V. Dependent statement continued: *nego*.

VI. Dependent statement continued.

VII. Purpose with *ut* and *ne*.

VIII. Purpose with *ut* and *ne*.

IX. Purpose continued: relative and subjunctive, *neve* and supine in *-um*.

X. Expressions of desire, non-dependent, and dependent with *ut*.

XI. Expressions of desire, non-dependent, and dependent with *ne*.

XII. 'Desire' continued.

XIII. *Cum* with past and past perfect subjunctive expressing 'attendant circumstances.'
The perfect participle in agreement with the object of the sentence.

XIV. Result.

XV. Direct and indirect reflexive.
Gerund (in ablative).

XVI. Dependent question and exclamation (with pres., past and 'future' subj.).
Gerund (in genitive).

XVII. Dependent question, etc., as in XVI.

XVIII. Dependent question and exclamation with perf. and past perf. subj.
Gerund (after *ad*).

XIX. Revision of dep. ques. and exclam.

XX. Open future conditions.
Gerund (before *causā*).

XXI. Conditions contrary to fact in past time.
Gerund-adjective of obligation (just begun).

XXII. Other types of condition.
The gerund-adjective of obligation is here developed in the *A* exercise.

XXIII. Gerund-adjective in its use as a passive participle.

XXIV. Revision.

## *Exercise* I

**A.**  1. In Livy's books many stories have been related.

2. The city of Rome was founded by Romulus.

3. Was not the manner of Romulus' death remarkable?

4. Numa was not at all like Romulus.

5. There was peace throughout Numa's reign.

**B.**  1. Romulus reigned at Rome for many years.

2. He is said to have gone up on high, wrapped in a thick cloud.

3. Proculus Iulius came forward and reported to the citizens Romulus' words. (Express by a *single* sentence.)

4. 'Rome,' said he, 'will one day be mistress of the world.'

5. Having said these words Proculus retired.

## *Exercise* II

**A.**  1. *In the course of the reign of Tullus Hostilius,* there took place a famous war. (Express the words italicized by a clause.)

2. There happened at the time to be three-brothers-born-at-a-birth in the two armies.

3. The Horatii were Romans and the Curiatii Albans.

4. These came forward into the centre between the two lines and engaged in combat. (Express by a single sentence.)

5. The Roman who was unhurt took to his heels.

**B.**  1. When the brothers had begun to fight, the two armies watched the combat in-great-anxiety as to the issue.

2. The three brothers had already taken up their arms and come forward.

3. Two of the Romans fell dead after wounding their opponents.

4. The three Albans, after bravely pursuing the Roman, were all killed by him.

5. 'Now that I have killed two of the brothers,' said the Roman, 'I shall soon despatch the third.'

## *Exercise* III

**A.** *No double or complex sentences to be used.*
1. Numa Pompilius' grandson was called Ancus Marcius.
2. He enrolled a fresh army and took many cities.
3. 'These times,' said he, 'are more suited to war than to peace.'
4. Finally he made a great effort and won a decisive victory.
5. Lucumo married in an Etruscan city and afterwards went to Rome.

**B.** 1. *Give the Latin for*: he settled at Rome; they returned to Corinth; we fled from Corinth; he is my grandson, my daughter's son.
2. The neighbouring peoples considered Ancus to be very lazy.
3. He, however, realized that the Latins wished to fight.
4. The Romans hoped that there would be peace throughout his reign.
5. They did not expect that he would wage wars.
6. Ancus, however, saw that to his times war was most appropriate.

## *Exercise* IV

**A.** 1. Tanaquil hoped that in a new town there would be scope for her husband.
2. Thinking that they had obtained a good omen they had high hopes.
3. When they had reached the city, they procured for themselves a house.
4. Lucumo, having given out a false name, tried-to-win the citizens to himself by many kindnesses.
5. When his fame had reached the palace, he was made guardian of the king's children.

**B.** 1. Tanaquil bade her husband take his property and depart to Rome.
2. His name was Lucumo, but he stated that he was called L. Tarquinius.
3. He determined to win the king's friendship.
4. *When the king died*, their guardian did not allow his sons to succeed him. (Express words italicized by a subordinate clause.)
5. He declared that he himself had learnt from an excellent teacher the laws of Rome.

## Exercise V

*A.* 1. It is said that Tarquinius Priscus drained the parts of the city which were in the neighbourhood of the Forum.

2. While this boy was asleep in the palace, many people saw a wonderful sight.

3. By their loud shouts they aroused the king and queen.

4. The queen forbade the slaves to put the flame out.

5. She drew Tarquinius aside and said that one day the boy would be king.

*B.* 1. Did you say that the king and queen did not betroth their daughter to Servius Tullius?

2. 'Undoubtedly,' said the sons of Ancus, 'this son-in-law of Tarquinius Priscus will one day be king.'

3. 'We know well that the kingdom will not come to us.'

4. They determined, therefore, to lay-a-plot against the king; for they realized that by his treachery they had been driven from their father's throne.

5. 'If he is put-out-of-the-way,' they said, 'we shall soon be able to seize the throne.'

## Exercise VI

*A.* *Single sentences to be used except in sentence 2.*

1. On appealing to the king the two shepherds were summoned to his presence.

2. They wanted both to speak at once, but the king's attendants bade them speak in turn.

3. While one of the two was telling his story, Tarquinius turned suddenly towards him.

4. The other then brought down an axe on the king's head and nearly killed him.

5. Tanaquil, however, a most wily woman, told the people that the king had (merely) been stunned by the blow.

*B.* 1. 'You shall soon see the king himself; meanwhile he has entrusted all (business) to his son-in-law.'

2. 'Be of good cheer, my friends,' said Tanaquil: 'his Majesty's wound is not a serious one.'

3. 'In the meantime Servius Tullius will perform all the duties of the king.'

4. By these words Tanaquil prevented the people from realizing that the king was already dead.

5. Servius then came forward and took his seat on the royal throne.

6. 'Some matters,' said he, 'I will decide myself: about others I will consult Tarquinius.'

## *Exercise* VII

*A.* 1. Although Servius Tullius had already pretended to be king, the people had not yet declared him as such.

2. He soon began to try to win to himself the sons of Tarquinius.

3. But though he gave his two daughters in marriage to them, still he did not secure peace.

4. The younger Tullia bade her husband seize the throne.

5. She bade him not be a coward.

6. 'I hope,' said she, 'that you will not merely hope for the position-of-king.'

*B.* 1. The younger Tullia held many secret consultations with Lucius, in order that she might secure his help.

2. Lucius married her in order that he might soon seize the throne.

3. 'I will give my husband no rest,' said Tullia, 'in order that our past crimes may not go-for-nothing.'

4. Servius' companions fled in order that they might not be arrested and put to death.

5. Lucius seized hold of Servius in order to fling him down the steps of the senate-house.

## *Exercise* VIII

*A.* 1. Tarquinius put to death those who had supported Servius Tullius.

2. When a council had been summoned, Turnus said that the king himself was not present.

3. At last the Latin chieftains said they would go home.

4. Tarquinius pretended to think that a plot was being laid against him by Turnus.

5. When his slaves were arrested, Turnus realized that he would soon be put to death, but he did not know that he would be drowned.

*B.* 1. The chief men of the Latins had come quickly in order to arrive at dawn.

2. The king, who had hardly turned up by sunset, said, in order to excuse himself, that he had brought-about-a-reconciliation-between a father and his son.

3. In order that they might murder Turnus, the guards arrested his slaves.

4. Others were preparing (to use) force in order that their master might not be taken.

5. In order that he might not escape, Turnus was put in chains.

6. In order that he himself might be safe, Tarquinius brought-about-the-ruin-of Turnus despite-his-innocence.

## *Exercise* IX

*A.* 1. 'In order,' said Tarquinius, 'that this temple may be worthy of the king of the gods, I will use public money for it.'

2. 'Which of us two,' said Arruns and Titus, 'will succeed-to the throne?'

3. In order that they might not understand Apollo gave a strange answer.

4. Titus and Arruns said that they did not understand the words of the oracle.

5. On hearing Apollo's answer Brutus stumbled and fell in order that he might be able to kiss the earth.

*B.* 1. 'I will build a temple,' said Superbus, 'that shall be both beautiful and famous.'

2. 'In order that I may be safe,' said Brutus, 'and may not be put-out-of-the-way, I shall pretend to be a fool.'

3. There appeared a portent that was to alarm even the king himself.

4. When Tarquinius sent his sons to the oracle to make enquiries, he gave them his nephew as a companion.

5. That they might not merely carry-out their father's instructions, they dared to ask Apollo another question.

## *Exercise* X

*A.* 1. Lucretia, who had married Collatinus and lived at Collatia, was an excellent wife.

2. She sent a messenger to her father to say that a dreadful thing had happened.

3. When her father and husband arrived, they promised to punish Sextus Tarquinius.

4. Hereupon Lucretia plunged a dagger into her heart and fell dead.

5. The gates of Rome were shut that Tarquinius might not enter.

6. So he went into exile in Etruria.

*B.* 1. 'Hasten to Collatia,' said Lucretia's father, 'for my daughter's messenger brings bad news.'

2. 'Carry her body,' said Brutus, 'down into the forum.'

3. 'Let brave men,' said Brutus, 'take up arms and defend their freedom.'

4. 'Brutus,' said those who stood round, 'is urging brave men to defend their freedom.'

5. Brutus urged the others to carry Lucretia's body down into the forum.

6. He entreated the Roman people to banish Lucius Tarquinius.

7. The messengers who had gone to the camp had already persuaded him to hasten to Rome.

8. When he got to Rome and found the gates shut, he did not ask to be admitted.

9. 'I do not choose,' said he, 'to crave admittance into the city over which I rule.'

10. 'I will go elsewhere and ask another king to help me.'

## *Exercise* XI

*A.* 1. 'I entreat you, Collatinus,' said Brutus, 'to free your fellow-citizens from this apprehension.'
   2. He urged him to bear away from Rome the very name of the tyrant.
   3. He promised that Collatinus' fellow-citizens would duly-deliver his property to him.
   4. 'Do you not remember,' said he, 'that with his help we procured-the-banishment-of the royal family?'
   5. 'Nevertheless let us urgently entreat him to quit Rome.'
   6. His father-in-law at last persuaded him to let-himself-be-influenced by the general wish.

*B.* 1. 'Let not the name of king,' they said, 'exist at Rome any longer.'
   2. 'Let not the royal family hinder (the exercise of) our freedom.'
   3. 'Do not you, L. Tarquinius Collatinus, oppose the unanimous-wish of your fellow-citizens.'
   4. Brutus entreated Collatinus not to go away in-a-hostile-spirit.
   5. Many urged him not to remain in the city any longer.
   6. Not even Sp. Lucretius recommended him not to resign his consulship.

## *Exercise* XII

*A.* 1. 'Those men,' said those who were watching, 'are collecting conveyances in which to take home the property of the royal family.'
   2. For the ambassadors sent by the king had urged that his property should be restored.
   3. They had not at first asked that he should return to Rome.
   4. Later on they entreated the young men not to allow the Tarquins to remain in exile.
   5. These suggestions did not displease them; for, being accustomed to live in regal style, they thought it would be dangerous to live without the protection of a king.

*B.* 1. The young men begged the king's emissaries not to speak openly of their new plans and not to allow their conversation to be overheard.

2. At last men were sent to arrest the traitors; but the ambassadors were not put to death, because international law forbade their punishment.

3. Therefore the Romans said, 'Do not remain longer in this city, but return at once to him who sent you.'

4. The senate had previously resolved that Tarquin's emissaries should take his property home.

5. When, however, the conspiracy had been crushed, they ordered that the property should *not* be restored.

## *Exercise* XIII

*A.* 1. The consuls set out from home and soon crushed the conspiracy.

2. They sent lictors to bind the young men to the stake.

3. On receiving the news of the punishment of the conspirators, Tarquinius realized that his hope had been baffled.

4. He entreated the people of Veii to render aid.

5. When Arruns caught sight of Brutus, he advanced in great rage.

6. The consul, after collecting the spoils, returned to Rome and conducted the funeral of his colleague.

*B.* 1. They bound the young men to the stake and beheaded them.

2. They stripped and scourged the conspirators.

3. They executed and buried the sons of Brutus.

4. When the consuls had taken their seats, all expressed pity for Brutus.

5. When Tarquinius was-making-a-tour-of the Etruscan cities, he stated that he was anxious to be avenged on his subjects.

6. When Arruns and Brutus were advancing furiously against one another, neither thought ( =was mindful) of himself.

## *Exercise* XIV

*A.* 1. The consul did not realize that the feelings of the populace were so fickle.

2. When P. Valerius began to build a house on an elevated spot, he fell under suspicion.

3. He therefore summoned and harangued an assembly of the people.

4. He mounted (a platform) to address the meeting and promised that his house should no longer be an obstacle to their freedom.

5. He then brought the timber down to level ground and set it up below the hill.

*B. Rule.*

Rules of sequence do not apply to clauses of result. At present you will only need to choose between the present, past and perfect subjunctive in these clauses. Use the present if the result applies to present time, e.g., *tam aeger heri fui ut hodie exire non possim.* To decide between the past and the perfect tenses, consider whether the past imperfect or the perfect indicative would be used if the contents of the result clause were expressed as a main clause: e.g., *tam aeger fui ut per aliquot dies vix quicquam ēsse possem* (*poteram* in the supposed main clause), contrasted with *tam aeger fui ut medicus adhibitus sit* (*adhibitus est* in the main clause).

1. The populace is always so fickle that no one is secure.

2. So lofty was (the situation of) this place that the people thought the consul's house would form an impregnable fortress.

3. This sight was so acceptable to them that they were willing to listen to the consul's speech.

4. These measures won for him such favour that he was given the name of Publicola.

5. Spurius Lucretius was so feeble that he could not perform the duties of a consul.

## *Exercise* XV

*A.* 1. When Lars Porsinna came against Rome with a hostile force, the senate tried to win the favour of the lower orders.

2. 'Let us procure corn,' they said, 'and afterwards sell it to the people at a low rate.'

3. 'Wealthy men at Rome have so much money now-a-days that they can easily pay a high rate-of-tax.'

4. So quickly did the enemy run down from it after capturing the Janiculum that the Romans threw down their arms and fled.

5. On the approach of the enemy Horatius Cocles and two others saved the city.

6. On hearing the crash of the broken bridge the Romans gave a loud shout.

*B.* *Rule.*

The reflexive pronoun *se* and its corresponding adjective *suus* must be used not only to refer to the subject of the sentence, clause or phrase in which it stands, but also to refer to the subject of the main clause in a subordinate clause which reflects the thought or will of that subject.

It must *not* be used in one half of a double subject to refer to the other half.

1. Tarquin persuaded Porsinna to help him.

2. The senate by ruling well on this occasion induced the people to aid them against Porsinna.

3. Horatius entreated his fellow-citizens not to betray the city by running away.

4. He urged them to break down the bridge and said that he would receive the enemy's attack in his own person.

5. When (only) a small part of the bridge remained, he told his comrades not to remain with him any longer.

6. In a loud voice he entreated the Tiber to lend him aid.

7. By jumping down into the river he saved himself.

8. Horatius Cocles and his comrades have become very famous.

## *Exercise* XVI

*A.* 1. Food at Rome was so scarce and dear that Porsinna hoped to take the city (simply) by sitting still.

2. C. Mucius begged the senate to let him cross the Tiber and enter the enemy's camp.

3. When he had set out from Rome and reached the Etruscan camp, he saw two men sitting there, dressed very much alike.

4. When he had killed the secretary instead of the king and was trying to escape, the king's guards arrested and dragged him back.

5. After his arrest he at once told Porsinna that he was a Roman citizen called Mucius.

*B.* 1. After this the Etruscans had no opportunity of roaming about all over the place.

2. The senate soon realized why Mucius wanted to enter the enemy's camp.

3. 'I am afraid,' said Mucius, 'to enquire which of these two men is Porsinna and which his secretary.'

4. 'For I do not want to disclose who I myself am.'

5. When Mucius thrust his hand into the fire, the king realized how worthless the body was in his eyes.

6. Porsinna did not know which of the 300 conspirators was going-to-kill him.

## *Exercise* XVII

*A.* 1. At first the guards asserted that the girls could not have escaped.

2. Cloelia, however, had persuaded the other female hostages to swim across the Tiber with her.

3. When she had brought them all safe back to Rome, the guards sent men to tell the king the truth.

4. What will Porsinna do? Will he not send ambassadors to demand the restoration of the hostages?

5. Will he not demand Cloelia's return (as) a guarantee of peace?

6. Surely he will not be so generous as to promise to send her back unharmed?

*B.* 1. Cloelia soon realized where the Etruscan camp was.

2. The guards wondered at first when Cloelia and the other girls were likely-to-return.

3. Cloelia had asked her companions whether they were willing to swim across the river with her.

4. The girls' parents were wondering whether they would (ever) see them again.

5. The hostages, when they were brought forward, asked whom Cloelia was likely-to-choose.

6. They are asking me whether this statue of a maiden sitting on a horse is still in existence.

## *Exercise* XVIII

*A.* 1. The ambassadors said that the Romans would not open their gates to the royal family.

2. They entreated Porsinna to let them remain free.

3. After this Tarquinius Superbus went into exile at Tusculum, where his son-in-law lived.

4. P. Valerius was so good a man that the matrons of Rome mourned for him for a whole year.

5. Porsinna demanded that Tarquinius should retire to another town.

6. In order that they may be courageous all men need liberty.

*B.* 1. Livy tells us what answer the senate gave to the ambassadors sent by Porsinna.

2. We do not know for certain why P. Valerius was given a public funeral.

3. Can you tell me why in Roman records there were so many inaccuracies as regards dates?

4. We marvelled-to-hear how many books Livy wrote.

5. After the appointment of a dictator the common people were more ready to obey.

6. It was not clear who was the first to be appointed dictator.

## *Exercise* XIX

*A.* 1. The Latins said that war could no longer be post-
poned.
   2. Postumius exhorted his men to fight with the utmost
courage.
   3. Such was the force of their onset that both Aebutius
and Mamilius were wounded.
   4. The band of exiles under the command of L. Tarquinius fought in order that they might recover the
property of which they had been deprived.
   5. The dictator bade the cavalry dismount and take
part in the engagement.
   6. Mamilius was so clearly-marked-out by his dress and
arms that Herminius easily recognized him.

*B.* 1. The Romans did not at first know for certain whether
the Tarquins were present in the Latin army.
   2. Can you tell me why this battle was so fiercely and
obstinately contested?
   3. They wanted to know when and why Aebutius
retired from the fight.
   4. I cannot tell you whether the master of the horse
or the dictator was the better man.
   5. When the cavalry understood what the dictator
wished them to do, they obeyed at once.
   6. We learnt how bravely the Romans and the Latins
fought at Lake Regillus.

## *Exercise* XX

*A.* 1. Tarquinius, after the defeat of the Latins, fled to
Aristodemus and died at Cumae.
   2. 'Let the patricians take up arms in order that the
Volscians may be defeated.'
   3. 'Let no one imprison a Roman citizen.'
   4. 'Now that a chance of fighting is given us, we will rout
the enemy and plunder their camp.'
   5. To fight well, soldiers, you need both arms and
courage.
   6. Menenius Agrippa entreated that the patricians and
the plebeians would not wage war against one
another.

*B.* 1. 'Unless we intervene,' said the consuls, 'the plebeians will refuse to enlist.'

2. If you obey us, we will not make war upon you.

3. 'If the Aequi invade our territory,' said the Latins, 'we will seek help from the Romans.'

4. 'If we disband this army,' said the patricians, 'we shall no longer be safe.'

5. 'If we strike,' said the plebeians, 'we shall not be led out to fight.'

6. In order to protect the Latins, the Romans sent one of their consuls against the Aequi.

## *Exercise* XXI

*A.* 1. 'If the Romans will allow it,' said the Latins, 'we will take up arms in defence of our lands.'

2. 'If,' said Marcius, 'I rout the Volscians, I shall gain great praise.'

3. Coriolanus asked why he saw plebeians in office at Rome.

4. He suggested that the plebs should secede on this occasion also.

5. Attius Tullius and Cn. Marcius induced the Volscians to appoint them commanders-in-chief.

6. We can readily understand why corn was so dear after the secession of the plebs.

*B.* 1. 'At what price,' said the senators, 'must the corn be sold to the people?'

2. 'This disgrace,' said Coriolanus, 'must not be endured longer than necessary.'

3. Had not Cn. Marcius been on guard on this occasion, the Volscians would have gained the victory.

4. Had not the town (of) Corioli been taken by him, Marcius would not have been called Coriolanus.

5. If the plebeians had stayed at home and cultivated the fields, there would have been no lack of corn.

6. The slaves would all have perished, had not a great quantity of corn been brought up from Sicily.

7. If Coriolanus had presented himself on the appointed day, perhaps he would not have gone into exile.

## *Exercise* XXII

*A.* 1. 'We must banish these plebeian magistrates,' said Coriolanus. (Say 'must be banished by us.')

2. We must send messengers to the enemy's camp to soften the heart of Coriolanus.

3. We must not admit these priests into our camp.

4. We must give these ambassadors a stern answer.

5. 'I must take my little boys with me,' said Volumnia.

6. If arms are lacking, we must defend our country with tears and prayers.

7. 'Before you kiss me,' said Veturia, 'tell me whether you are my son or a public enemy.'

*B.* 1. 'If you *were* my son, you would not now be attacking your native country.'

2. 'If a premature death *were to be* the lot of your sons, would you not be utterly wretched?'

3. 'If these children were to become slaves, they would suffer many hardships' ('many and bad things').

4. 'If you were a good man, you would not be obstinate in the face of women's tears.'

5. Had not his mother addressed him in stern words, Coriolanus would not have yielded.

## *Exercise* XXIII

*A.* 1. The Romans would have retreated, had not the consul barred the way with his shield.

2. If we wish to be worthy of the name of Fabii, we must fire the courage of our troops.

3. Marcus asked whether the soldiers had taken an oath to return to the camp as fugitives.

4. If we were to send and tell the consuls the position of affairs, perhaps they would return to the camp.

5. Were we not (members) of the Fabian family, we should not be such brave men.

6. If they post soldiers at all the gates, they will bar the road to the enemy.

*B.* Express phrases or clauses of 'purpose' by *ad*, etc., in the first three sentences, and by *causa*, etc., in the last three.

1. Quintus Fabius set out to defeat the Volscians and secured a great quantity of booty.

2. In order to rouse the troops M. Fabius addressed them in stern words.

8. In order that he might restore the line Manlius, who had been seriously wounded, came forward and showed himself.

4. In order to carry the whole line with them, Caeso Fabius and his brother dashed forward to the front.

5. They returned in a body to renew the fight.

6. In order to open a path for the enemy, men hastily removed the consul's body.

## *Exercise* XXIV (*A* and *B*)

1. The consul said that they needed neither the money nor the soldiers of the state.

2. Caeso Fabius recommended the senate to give-their-attention-to other wars and leave the Veientes to them.

8. 'No-one-member of our family is to be despised,' said he.

4. 'If this family assumes a burden that belongs to the whole state, the honour of Rome will be secure.'

5. 'We hope,' said the by-standers, 'that these men will soon be restored to their parents in safety.'

6. This spot seemed suitable for the laying of an ambush.

7. The Fabii had conceived such a contempt for the enemy that these easily defeated them by a trick.

8. When the Fabii sighted the cattle, they ran down to seize them.

9. If the Fabii had not thought their arms invincible, they would not all have perished on one day.

10. If 306 men out of one family were to be killed in one battle, we should consider the family to be very unfortunate.

# LATIN-ENGLISH VOCABULARY

**N.B.** 1. WORDS *occurring in the* OVID *extracts as well as in the* LIVY *are included: the former are distinguished by* ROMAN NUMERALS, *the latter by* ARABIC. *Words occurring in* OVID *only should be looked for in the* SEPARATE VOCABULARY.

2. *The* ARABIC NUMERALS *indicate the first occurrence of a word in a particular chapter. Where more than one reference is given, the word has different meanings or shades of meaning.*

3. VERBS *which take an object infinitive, phrase or clause are here described as transitive, i.e. used transitively.*

4. *Long vowels are not marked in the ordinary endings and most common stems of nouns, adjectives and verbs.*

**a, ab**, prep. followed by ablative, *by*, 1: *from*, 5; **a tergo**, *in the rear*, 15.

**abdico**, -are, -avi, -atum, vb. tr.; **abdico me magistratu**, *I resign an office*, 11.

**abdo**, -dere, -didi, -ditum, vb. tr. *conceal*, 8.

**abdūco**, -ere, -duxi, -ductum, vb. tr. *draw aside*, 5.

**abeo**, -ire, -ii, -itum, vb. intr. *go away*, 1.

**abnuo**, -ere, -ui, vb. tr. *refuse*, 9.

**abrogo**, -are, -avi, -atum, vb. tr. *take away*; **abrogo alicui magistratum**, *I take away an office from someone*, 10.

**absens**, gen. absentis, adj. *absent, in absence*, 8.

**absolvo**, -ere, -solvi, -solūtum, vb. tr. *free from* (an accusation), 14.

**abstergeo**, -ere, -tersi, -tersum, vb. tr. *wipe off*, 6.

**absum**, -esse, -fui, vb. intr. *be absent*, 10.

**ac, atque**, coordinating conjunction, *and*, 4.

**accendo**, -ere, -cendi, -censum, vb. tr. *kindle*, 16.

**accidit**, -ere, -cidit, vb. intr. *happen*, 12.

**accio**, -ire, -ivi, -itum, vb. tr. *summon*, 6.

**accipio**, -ere, -cēpi, -ceptum, vb. tr. *accept, receive*, 3: *obtain*, 4.

**acies**, aciei, noun fem. *battle-line*, 2: *pitched battle*, 3: *field of battle*, 13.

**ad**, prep. followed by accus., *to*, 2: *at* (**ad rem**), 5: *in answer to* (with **respondeo**), 7: *until* (**ad posterum diem**), 8: *with a view to* (**ad id**), 9: *to face* (**ad crimen**), 14: *on, near* (**ad alterum cornu**), (**ad lacum Regillum**), 19; **ad unum**, *to a man*, 24.

**addo,** -ere, -didi, -ditum, vb. tr. *place near, send with,* 9.

**addūco,** -ere, -duxi, -ductum, vb. tr. *lead into* (with **in**): in pass. *fall a victim to,* 14.

**adeō,** advb. *so, to such an extent,* 14.

**adeo,** -ire, -ii, -itum, vb. tr. *approach,* 16.

**adfecto,** -are, -avi, -atum, vb. tr. *aspire to,* 14.

**adficio,** -ere, -fēci, -fectum, vb. tr.; **maestitiā adfectus,** *distressed,* 2: **summā laude adfectus est,** *was highly commended,* 21.

**adflīgo,** -ere, -flixi, -flictum, vb. tr. *dash down, distress,* 5.

**adgredior,** -i, -gressus, vb. tr. *attack,* 2.

**adhortor,** -ari, -atus, vb. tr. *encourage,* 19.

**adipiscor,** -i, adeptus, vb. tr. *obtain,* 9.

**aditus,** -us, noun masc. *approach,* 15.

**adiuvo,** -are, -iūvi, -iūtum, vb. tr. *help,* 13.

**adloquor,** -i, -locūtus, vb. tr. *address, harangue,* 6.

**administro,** -are, -avi, -atum, vb. tr. *administer, govern,* 8.

**admīrātio,** -onis, noun fem. *surprise,* 11.

**admīror,** -ari, -atus, vb. tr. *wonder at, wonder to see or hear,* 16.

**admoveo,** -ere, -mōvi, -mōtum, vb. tr. *bring up to,* 19.

**adorior,** -iri, -ortus, vb. tr. *attack,* 19.

**adprobo,** -are, -avi, -atum, vb. tr. *approve of,* 16.

**adsuesco,** -ere, -suēvi, -suētus, vb. intr. *grow accustomed,* 12.

**adsum,** -esse, -fui, vb. intr. *be present,* 8 : *be at hand,* 15.

**adsūmo,** -ere, -sumpsi, -sumptum, vb. tr. *associate with oneself,* 12.

**adulescens,** -entis, noun masc. *young man,* 12.

**adveho,** -ere, -vexi, -vectum, vb. tr. *bring up,* 21; **equo advectus,** *riding up,* 23.

**advenio,** -ire, -vēni, -ventum, vb. intr. *arrive, turn up,* 8.

**adversus,** prep. followed by accus. *against,* 2.

**advoco,** -are, -avi, -atum, vb. tr. *summon,* 8.

**advolo,** -are, -avi, -atum, vb. intr. *fly towards, hasten to,* 19.

**aedes,** aedis, noun fem. sing. *temple,* 19: plur. *house,* 6.

**aedificium,** -i, noun neut. *building,* 21.

**aedifico,** -are, -avi, -atum, vb. tr. *build,* 9.

**aegrē,** aegrius, aegerrimē, advb.; **aegre fero,** *take hardly, resent,* 8.

**aes,** aeris, noun neut. *bronze;* **aes alienum,** *debt* (other people's money), 20.

**aetas,** -atis, noun fem. *age,* 2.

**ager,** agri, noun masc. *field, territory,* 19; plur. *lands,* 7.

**agmen,** -inis, noun neut. *troop, band,* 7; **quadrato agmine,** *in order of battle,* 13: *troops in marching order* (**agmini**

hostium), 19: *marching order* (agmine **instructam**), 24.

**agnosco**, -ere, -nŏvi, -nitum, vb. tr. *recognize*, 13.

**ago**, -ere, ēgi, actum, vb. tr. *drive*, 23: *do*, 9; **regnum agere**, *spend one's reign*, 3: *treat of, dwell upon*, 18; **gratias agere**, *return thanks*, 24; **actum est de**, *it is all over with*, 24.

**agrestis**, -e, adj.; **agrestes**, *country people*, 24.

**aliās**, advb. *at another time*, 15.

**aliēnus**, -a, -um, adj. *belonging to others*, 20.

**aliō**, advb. *elsewhere, in another direction*, 9.

**aliquamdiŭ**, advb. *for some time*, 3.

**aliquantum**, -i, noun of quantity, *a considerable amount*, 2; **aliquanto**, abl., qualifies a comparative in 19 and 21, *considerably*.

**aliquot**, adj. indeclinable, *several*, 6.

**aliquotiens**, advb. *on several occasions*, 24.

**aliter**, advb. *in other ways, differently*, 18: *otherwise*, v.

**alius**, -a, -ud, gen. alius, adj. and pron. *another*; **alius super alium**, *one on the top of another*, 2; plur. **alia ...alia**, *some things...other things*, 6.

**alo**, -ere, alui, altum, vb. tr. *nourish, bring up*, 22.

**altē**, advb. *deeply, deep*, 6.

**alter**, -era, -erum, gen. al-

terius, adj. and pron. *one of two, the other of two*, 2.

**altus**, -a, -um, adj. *high*, 4.

**ambo**, -ae, -o, adj. and pron. *both*, 6.

**āmens**, amentis, adj. *distraught*, 22.

**amīcitia**, -ae, noun fem. *friendship*, 4.

**amīcus**, -a, -um, adj. and noun, *friendly*, 7: *friend*, 10.

**āmitto**, -ere, -mīsi, -missum, vb. tr. *lose*, 11.

**amplector**, -i, -plexus, vb. tr. *embrace*, 4.

**amplexus**, -us, noun masc. *embrace*, 22.

**an**, interrog. advb.; **utrum ...an**, *whether...or*, 22.

**anceps**, -cipitis, adj. *twofold*, 19.

**ango**, -ere, vb. tr. *distress, vex*, 14.

**anguis**, -is, noun common, *snake*, 9.

**animadverto**, -ere, -ti, -sum, vb. tr. *notice, remark*, 19.

**animus**, noun masc. *mind*, 7: *courage*, 19; **in animo habere**, *have in mind, intend*, 4; **bono animo esse**, *be of good cheer*, 6; **in animum induco**, *conceive the idea of*, 13: *make up one's mind to*, 18; **animi**, plur. *feelings*, 12.

**annōna**, -ae, noun fem. *corn-supply*, 15: *price of corn*, 21.

**annus**, -i, noun masc. *year*, 5.

**ante**, prep. foll. by accus. *before*, 8; advb. v.

**anteā**, advb. *before*, 1.

**antecēdo**, -cedere, -cessi, -cessum, vb. intr. *go in front*, 13,

**antīquus**, -a, -um, adj. *ancient*, 1.

**anxius**, -a, -um, adj. *distressful*, 9.

**aperio**, -ire, -ui, -tum, vb. tr. *open, reveal*, 16.

**apertē**, advb. *openly, avowedly*, 12.

**apparātus**, -us, noun masc. *magnificent preparation, pomp*, 13.

**appāreo**, -ere, -ui, vb. intr. *appear, be seen*, 5.

**appāritor**, -oris, noun masc. *attendant*, 6.

**appello**, -are, -avi, -atum, vb. tr. *call*, 2: *appeal to*, 6.

**aptus**, -a, -um, adj. followed by the dative, *suited*, 3.

**apud**, preposition foll. by the accus. *at the house of*: *in the presence of*, 4: *among*, apud omnes, 5: *in*, apud alios auctores, 18.

**aqua**, -ae, noun fem. *water*, 5.

**aquila**, -ae, noun fem. *eagle*, 4.

**āra**, -ae, noun fem. *altar*, 8.

**arceo**, -ere, -ui, vb. tr. *ward off, prevent*, 5.

**arcesso**, -ere, -ivi, -itum, vb. tr. *send for*, 10.

**ardeo**, -ere, arsi, arsum, vb. intr. *be on fire, be eager*, 7.

**ardor**, -oris, noun masc. *eagerness, enthusiasm*, 19.

**arma**, -orum, noun neuter plur. *arms, weapons*, 2.

**armo**, -are, -avi, -atum, vb. tr. *furnish with arms*, 8.

**arripio**, -ere, -ripui, -reptum, vb. tr. *snatch up*, 7.

**ars**, artis, noun fem. *art*, 5.

**arx**, arcis, noun fem. *citadel*, 14.

**asporto**, -are, -avi, -atum, vb. tr. *carry off*, 12.

**at**, coordinating conj. *but*, 23.

**atque**. See ac.

**atrox**, -ocis, adj. *fearful*, 7: *harsh*, 21 : *fiercely contested*, 19.

**auctor**, -oris, noun common, *author*, 18.

**auctōritas**, -atis, noun fem. *authority, influence*, 8.

**audācia**, -ae, noun fem. *courage, impudence*, 7.

**audeo**, -ere, ausus, vb. tr. *dare, have the courage to*, 7.

**audio**, -ire, -ivi, -itum, vb. tr. *hear: listen to*, 8.

**aufero**, -ferre, abstuli, ablātum, vb. tr. *carry off, bear away, remove*, 11.

**aufugio**, -ere, -fūgi, vb. intr. *flee away*, 2.

**augeo**, -ere, auxi, auctum, vb. tr. *increase, build up*, 1.

**augurium**, -i, noun neuter, *omen*, 4.

**aureus**, -a, -um, adj. *golden*, 9.

**aurum**, -i, noun neuter, *gold*, 8.

**aut**, coordinating conjunction, *or*, 7; aut...aut, *either ...or*, 20.

**autem**, coordinating conjunction, *but, however*, 2.

**auxilium**, -i, noun neuter, *help*, 11.

**āverto**, -ere, -ti, -sum, vb. tr. *turn away*, 6.

**avidē**, advb. *eagerly*, 13.

**avunculus**, -i, noun masc. *uncle*, 9.

**avus**, -i, noun masc. *grandfather*, 3.

**baculum**, -i, noun neuter, *stick, staff*, 9.

**bellātor**, -oris, noun masc. *warrior, fighting man*, 10.

**bellum**, -i, noun neuter, *war*, 1.

**bene**, melius, optime, advb. *well*, 15.

**beneficium**, -i, noun neuter, *act of kindness*, 4.

**benignē**, benignius, benignissime, advb. *kindly*, 21.

**benignitas**, -atis, noun fem. *kindness*, 4.

**benignus**, -a, -um, adj. *kind*, 4.

**bis**, advb. *twice*, 2.

**bonus**, -a, -um, melior, optimus, adj. *good*, 4. The neuter plur. *bona* is used as a noun meaning *goods, property*, 4.

**brachium**, -i, noun neuter, *arm*, 19.

**brevī**, equivalent to an advb. *shortly, in a short time*, 16.

**brevis**, -e, adj. *brief*, 3.

**cado**, -ere, cecidi, cāsum, vb. intr. *fall*, 9; ad inritum cadere, *be baffled*, 13.

**caedes**, -is, noun fem. *slaughter*, 21.

**caedo**, -ere, cecīdi, caesum, vb. tr. *beat*, 13: *cut down*, 19.

**caelum**, -i, noun neuter, *sky, heaven*, 1.

**calcar**, -is, noun neuter, *spur*, 10.

**campus**, -i, noun masc. *plain*, 20.

**capio**, -ere, cēpi, captum, vb. trans. *take up*, 2: *capture*, 3; fugam capere, *take to flight*,

2: consilium capere, *form a plan*, 24.

**captīvus**, -a, -um, adj. and noun, *captive*, 22.

**capto**, -are, -avi, -atum, vb. tr. *try to entrap*, 24.

**caput**, -itis, noun neuter, *head*, 1.

**cāritas**, -atis, noun fem. *affection*, 8: *dearness* (of price), 16.

**castra**, -orum, noun neuter plur. *camp*, 2.

**cāsus**, -us, noun masc. *fall*, 23. The abl. casu is used to mean *accidentally* in 24.

**catēna**, -ae, noun fem. *chain*, 8.

**causa**, -ae, noun fem. *excuse*, 20; indictā causā, *without having pleaded his cause*, 8. The abl. is used as a preposition, preceded by a genitive, in the meaning *for the sake of, with a view to*, 19.

**cēdo**, -ere, cessi, cessum, vb. intr. *retire, yield*, 15.

**celeritas**, -atis, noun fem. *speed*, 10.

**celeriter**, celerius, celerrime, advb. *quickly*, 6.

**cēlo**, -are, -avi, -atum, vb. tr. *conceal*, 6.

**cēna**, -ae, noun fem. *dinner*, 12.

**certāmen**, -inis, noun neuter, *conflict*, 13.

**certātim**, advb. *in a quarrelsome manner*, 6.

**certo**, -are, -avi, -atum, vb. intr. *fight: vie with*, 4.

**certus**, -a, -um, adj. *fixed*, 8; **pro certo habeo**, *regard* as *settled, feel sure, know well,* 5.

cēteri, -ae, -a, adj. and noun, *the rest,* 6. Rare in singular, cetera turba, v.

cēterum, coord. conj. *but,* 12.

cieo, -ere, civi, citus, vb. tr. *rouse*; proelium or pugnam ciere, *cheer on the fight,* 19.

circā, advb. and prep. (foll. by accus.), *round about,* 6: *in the neighbourhood of,* 5.

circumdo, -dare, -dedi, -datum, vb. tr. *put round* (with accus. and dat.), 16.

circumeo, -ire, -ii, -itum, vb. tr. *make the round of,* 13.

circumfero, -ferre, -tuli, -lātum, vb. tr. *carry round*: in passive, *ring round* (of a shout), 24.

circumfundo, -fundere, -fūdi, -fūsum, vb. tr. *pour or shed round,* 6.

circummitto, -mittere, -mīsi, -missum, vb. tr. *send round,* 24.

circumsaepio, -ire, -saepsi, -saeptum, vb. tr. *hedge about,* 8.

circumsisto, -sistere, -steti, vb. tr. *take one's stand round,* 8.

circumvenio, -ire, -vēni, -ventum, vb. tr. *surround,* 2.

citātus, -a, -um, perf. part. of cito, used to mean *at full speed,* 15.

cito, -are, -avi, -atum, vb. tr. *summon,* 7.

cīvis, -is, noun common,

citizen, 1: *fellow-citizen,* 11: *subject,* 13.

cīvitas, -atis, noun fem. *state,* 1.

clādes, -is, noun fem. *disaster,* 16.

clam, advb. *secretly,* 8.

clāmor, -oris, noun masc. *shout,* 5.

clārus, -a, -um, adj. *famous, distinguished,* 2.

claudo, -ere, clausi, clausum, vb. tr. *shut, shut up, shut upon* (with dat.), 10.

clīvus, -i, noun masc. *slope, hill,* 14.

cloāca, -ae, noun fem. *sewer,* 5.

coemo, -ere, -ēmi, -emptum, vb. tr. *buy up,* 21.

coeo, -ire, -ii, -itum, vb. intr. *throng together,* 24.

coepi, coepisse, vb. used as the perf. tense of incipio, *begin,* when an inf. follows, 3.

coerceo, -ere, -ui, -itum, vb. tr. *restrain,* 6.

cōgitātio, -onis, noun fem. *thought, reflection,* 4.

cognātus, -i, noun masc. *relative,* 10.

cognōmen, -inis, noun neuter. The third name, often used almost as a nickname, e.g. Superbus in 8.

cognosco, -ere, -nōvi, -nitum, vb. tr. *get to know,* 23.

cōgo, -ere, coēgi, coactum, vb. tr. *compel,* 15.

cohors, -hortis, noun fem. *troop, band,* 19.

collēga, -ae, noun masc. *colleague,* 11.

collis, -is, noun masc. *hill,* 14,

colo, -ere, -ui, cultum, vb. tr. *cultivate*, 1: *treat*, 21.

columna, -ae, noun fem. *pillar*, 9.

comes, -itis, noun common, *companion*, 7.

cōmitas, -atis, noun fem. *kindness, courtesy*, 4.

comitia, -orum, noun neuter plur. *election*, 14.

comitor, -ari, -atus, vb. tr. *accompany*, 24.

commigro, -are, -avi, -atum, vb. intr. *remove* (with all one's property), 4.

committo, -ere, -mīsi, -missum, vb. tr. *entrust*, 6.

commūnio, -ire, -ivi, -itum, vb. tr. *fortify strongly*, 20.

commūnis, -e, adj. *common, universal*, 9.

comparo, -are, -avi, -atum, vb. tr. *procure, secure*, 4.

compello,-ere,-puli,-pulsum, vb. tr. *drive (together)*, 16.

complōrātio, -onis, noun fem. *violent lament*, 6.

comprehendo, -ere, -di, -sum, vb. tr. *arrest*, 6.

comprimo, -ere, -pressi, -pressum, vb. tr. *repress*, 20.

cōnātus, -us, noun masc. *attempt*, 16.

concēdo, -ere, -cessi, -cessum, vb. tr. *grant, concede*, 20.

concieo, -ciere, -civi, -citum, vb. tr. *arouse*, 10.

concilio, -are, -avi, -atum, vb. tr. *win over*, 4.

concilium, -i, noun neut. *council*, 8.

concito, -are, -avi, -atum,

vb. tr. *rouse up, spur on* (with calcaribus), 10.

conclāmo, -are, -avi, -atum, vb. intr. *cry aloud*, 10.

concordia, -ae, noun fem. *harmony*, 20.

concors, -cordis, adj. *harmonious*, 15.

concurro, -ere, -curri, -cursum, vb. intr. *flock together*, 10: *run together* (in conflict), 13.

concursus, -us, noun masc. *running together, onset*, 2: *rally*, 19.

condemno, -are, -avi, -atum, vb. tr. *condemn*, 8.

condo, -ere, -didi, -ditum, vb. tr. *found*, 1.

confero, -ferre, -tuli, -lātum, vb. tr. literally *bring together*. In 8 used reflexively, *betake oneself*: *contribute*, 15: with signa, *fight a pitched battle*, 20: with consilia, *consult together*, 21.

confertus, -a, -um, perf. ptc. of confercio, *close-packed*, 16.

confestim, advb. *immediately*, 8.

conflīgo, -ere, -flixi, -flictum, vb. intr. *fight*, 19.

congero,-ere,-gessi,-gestum, vb. tr. *heap together, pile up*, 8.

conglobo, -are, -avi, -atum, vb. tr. *mass together*, 23.

conicio, -icere, -iēci, -iectum, vb. tr. *fling, hurl*, 15; in vincla conicere, *imprison*, 12.

cōnītor, -nīti, -nīsus or -nixus, vb. intr. *make a great effort*, 3.

**coniunx**, -iugis, noun fem. *wife*, 4 (rarely masc. *husband*).

**coniūrāti**, -orum, noun masc. plur. *conspirators*, 12.

**coniūrātio**, -onis, noun fem. *conspiracy*, 20.

**coniūro**, -are, -avi, -atum, vb. tr. *take an oath together, conspire*, 16.

**conloquor**, -loqui, -locūtus, vb. tr. *converse, confer*, 12.

**cōnor**, -ari, -atus, vb. tr. *try*, 6.

**conscrībo**, -scribere, -scripsi, -scriptum, vb. tr. *enrol*, 3. The perf. ptc. is commonly added as an epithet to **patres**, *senators*, 24.

**consensus**, -us, noun masc. *general consent*, 4.

**consequor**, -sequi, -secutus, vb. tr. *overtake*, 2.

**consero**, -ere, -serui, -sertum, vb. tr. *join together*; with **manus**, *engage in combat*, 2.

**consīdo**, -ere, -sēdi, -sessum, vb. intr. *sit down*, 2 : *settle*, 3.

**consilium**, -i, noun neut. *plan, intention*, 7 ; *judgment*, 21.

**consisto**, -ere, -stiti, verb intr. *take one's stand*, 16.

**conspectus**, -us, noun masc. *sight*, 5.

**conspicio**, -ere, -spexi, -spectum, vb. tr. *catch sight of*, 24.

**conspicor**, -ari, -atus, vb. tr. *catch sight of*, 19.

**constat**, 3rd sing. of **constare**, used impersonally, *it is established, it is agreed*, 18.

**consterno**, -are, -avi, -atum, vb. tr. *terrify, dismay*, 22.

**constituo**, -ere, -ui, -ūtum, vb. tr. *determine*, 4.

**consul**, -is, noun masc. *consul* (one of the two highest magistrates chosen annually to govern the state after the expulsion of the kings), 10.

**consulātus**, -us, noun masc. *office of consul, consulship*, 11.

**consulo**, -ere, -sului, -sultum, vb. tr. *consult, take the advice of*, 6.

**consultum**, -i, noun neut. *decree*; **senatus consultum**, *decree of the senate*, 24.

**consūmo**, -ere, -sumpsi, -sumptum, vb. tr. *consume, spend*, 12.

**consurgo**, -ere, -surrexi, -surrectum, vb. intr. *rise together*, 24.

**contemno**, -ere, contempsi, contemptum, vb. tr. *despise, conceive contempt for*, 24.

**contemptim**, advb. *contemptuously*, 21.

**contemptus**, -us, noun masc. *contempt, the state of being despised*, 9.

**continens**, -entis, pres. ptc. of **contineo**, *holding together, continuous*, 24.

**contingo**, -ere, -tigi, -tactum, vb. tr. *touch*, 9.

**continuus**, -a, -um, adj. *continuous, successive*, 23.

**contio**, -onis, noun fem. *meeting, assembly*, 11.

**contrā**, prep. foll. by accus. *against*, 7.

contrārius, -a, -um, adj.
*opposite, from opposite directions*, 13.

convallis, -is, noun fem.
*valley* (enclosed on all sides), 5.

conveho, -ere, -vexi, -vectum,
vb. tr. *bring together, collect*,
8.

convenio, -ire, -vēni, -ven-
tum, vb. intr. *come to-
gether, assemble*, 7.

convenit, 3rd sing. of con-
venire used impersonally,
*it is agreed*, 6 and 24.

conventus, -us, noun masc.
*meeting*, 8.

converto, -ere, -ti, -sum, vb.
tr. *turn, attract*, 6.

convoco, -are, -avi, -atum,
vb. tr. *call together, summon*, 7.

coorior, -oriri, -ortus, vb.
intr. *arise, break forth*, 1.

cōpiae, -arum, noun fem.
plur. *forces, troops*, 8: *resources*, 18.

cor, cordis, noun neut. *heart*,
10.

cōram, advb. *in person*,
23.

corneus, -a, -um, adj. *made
of horn*, 9.

cornu, -us, noun neut. *horn*,
*wing* (of army), 19.

corpus, -oris, noun neut.
*body*, 2.

corrumpo, -ere, -rūpi, -rup-
tum, vb. tr. *spoil, bribe*, 8.

corruo, -ere, -rui, vb. intr.
*fall together, collapse*, 2.

crātis, -is, noun fem. *hurdle*,
8.

crēdo, -ere, -didi, -ditum,

vb. tr. and intr. *believe*,
1.

creo, -are, -avi, -atum, vb. tr.
*make, elect*, 8: *appoint*, 11.

cresco, -ere, crēvi, crētum,
vb. intr. *increase*, 23.

crīmen, -inis, noun neut. *accusation*, 8.

cubiculum, -i, noun neut.
*room*, 10.

culter, -tri, noun masc.
*knife*, 10.

cultus, -us, noun masc. *manner of life*, 5.

cum, conjunction, *when suddenly*, 2: *when*, 13.

cum, preposition foll. by abl.
*together with, attended by*, 1.

cuncti, -ae, -a, adj. or pron.
*all*, 15.

cūr, interr. advb. *why?* 21.

cūra, -ae, noun fem. *care*, 15:
*anxiety, apprehension*, 2:
*responsibility*, 3.

cūrātio, -onis, noun fem.
*care, aid*, 19.

cūria, -ae, noun fem. *senate-
house*, 7.

cūro, -are, -avi, -atum, vb. tr.
*care for, give attention to*, 24.

cursus, -us, noun masc.
*running*, 2.

custōs, -ōdis, noun common,
*guard*, 8.

dē, prepos. foll. by abl.
*down from, concerning*, 1;
de publico, *from public
funds*, 18; poenas sumere
de, *exact a penalty from*, 10;
victoriam reportare de,
20.

dēbello, -are, -avi, -atum,
vb. intr. *finish off a war*, 20.

dēcēdo, -ere, -cessi, -cessum, vb. intr. *depart, retire,* 20.

dēcerno, -ere, -crēvi, -crētum, vb. tr. and intr. *decide,* 6: *resolve, decree,* 12.

decet, impersonal vb. of 2nd conj. *it is becoming to, it befits,* 23.

dēclāro, -are, -avi, -atum, vb. tr. *declare, proclaim publicly,* 7.

decoro, -are, -avi, -atum, vb. tr. *adorn,* 13.

dēcurro, -ere, -curri, -cursum, vb. intr. *run down,* 15.

decus, -oris, noun neut. *glory, honour,* 13.

dēdecus, -oris, noun neut. *disgrace,* 5.

dēdo, -ere, -didi, -ditum, vb. tr. *surrender,* 17.

dēdūco, -ere, -duxi, -ductum, vb. tr. *withdraw,* 16.

dēfendo, -ere, -fendi, -fensum, vb. tr. *defend, protect,* 20.

dēfero, -ferre, -tuli, -lātum, vb. tr. *carry down,* 10: *bring down,* 14; defero ad, *report to,* 12.

dēfīgo, -ere, -fixi, -fixum, vb. tr. *fix in, plunge,* 2: *fasten upon,* 13.

dēicio, -ere, -iēci, -iectum, vb. tr. *bring down upon,* 6: *cast down,* 7.

deinceps, advb. *one after the other, successively,* 1.

deinde, advb. *then, secondly,* 1.

dēlābor, -i, -lapsus, vb. intr. *glide down,* 1.

dēlībero, -are, -avi, -atum, vb. intr. *deliberate, consider,* 12.

dēligo, -are, -avi, -atum, vb. tr. *bind,* 13.

dēligo, -ere, -lēgi, -lectum, vb. tr. *choose,* 6.

dēmando, -are, -avi, -atum, vb. tr. *entrust,* 3.

dēmergo, -ere, -mersi, -mersum, vb. tr. *drown,* 8.

dēmigro, -are, -avi, -atum, vb. intr. *depart, withdraw,* 15.

dēmum, advb. *at last:* used to emphasise some such word as tum, 6.

dēnique, advb. *finally, at last,* 3.

dens, dentis, noun masc. *tooth,* 20.

densus, -a, -um, adj. *thick,* 1.

dēposco, -ere, -poposci, vb. tr. *demand,* 17.

dēprehendo, -ere, -ndi, -nsum, vb. tr. *catch,* 12.

dērigo, -ere, -rexi, -rectum, vb. tr. *direct against* (with in), 13.

descendo, -ere, -ndi, -nsum, vb. intr. *go down,* 6; *dismount,* 19.

dēsero, -ere, -ui, -tum, vb. tr. *abandon,* 15.

dēsīderium, -i, noun neut. *regret* (for what one has lost), 1.

dēsilio, -ire, -silui, -sultum, vb. intr. *jump down,* 15.

dēsisto, -ere, destiti, vb. intr. *cease,* 6.

dēspondeo, -ere, -ndi, -nsum, vb. tr. *betroth,* 5.

dēstituo, -ere, -ui, -ūtum, vb. tr. *leave all alone, forsake,* 16.

**dēsum**, -esse, -fui, vb. intr. *be lacking*, 11.

**dēterreo**, -ere, -ui, -itum, vb. tr. *frighten away, deter*, 19.

**dētrūdo**, -ere, -trūsi, -trūsum, vb. tr. *push down*, 15.

**deus**, dei (nom. plur. di, 7; gen. plur. **deum**), noun masc. *god*, 6.

**dēversōrium**, -i, noun neut. *lodging*, 8.

**dēvinco**, -ere, -vīci, -victum, vb. tr. *win a complete victory over, completely defeat*, 23.

**dexter**, dextra, dextrum, adj. *right*, 16: *on the right hand*, 24.

**dextra**, -ae, noun fem. *right hand*, 16.

**dīco**, -ere, dixi, dictum, vb. tr. *say*, 1. Used in 6 for *speak*; **diem dico**, *appoint a day for the trial of*, 21; *call*, ɪ (**dixere paludem**); *promise*, ɪɪ (**dictas opes**).

**dictātor**, -oris, noun masc. *dictator*: the highest Roman magistrate, elected in emergency, 18.

**dictatūra**, -ae, noun fem. *the office of dictator*, 20.

**dictum**, -i, noun neut. *order*, 18.

**dies**, diei, noun both masc. and fem. in Livy, 6. Generally fem. of a fixed day, e.g. 8; **in dies**, *day by day*, 7.

**differo**, -ferre, distuli, dilātum, vb. tr. *postpone*, 8.

**dīgero**, -ere, -gessi, -gestum, vb. tr. *set in order, state definitely*, 18.

**dignitas**, -atis, noun fem. *dignity, worth*, 11.

**dignus**, -a, -um, adj. used with abl. *worthy of*, 9.

**dīmico**, -are, -avi, -atum, vb. intr. *fight*, 14.

**dīmitto**, -ere, -mīsi, -missum, vb. tr. *let go*, 16: *disband*, 20: *send in different directions*, 21.

**dīrimo**, -ere, -ēmi, -emptum, vb. tr. *break off, dissolve*, 8.

**dīripio**, -ere, -ripui, -reptum, vb. tr. *plunder*, 12.

**discēdo**, -ere, -cessi, -cessum, vb. intr. *depart*, 11.

**disco**, -ere, didici, vb. tr. *learn*, 4.

**dispār**, -paris, adj. *unlike*, 2.

**displiceo**, -ere, -ui, vb. intr., used with dat. *displease, be unwelcome to*, 12.

**disputo**, -are, -avi, -atum, vb. intr. *dispute, argue*, 9.

**dissimilis**, -e, -ior, -illimus, adj. *unlike*, 1.

**dissipo**, -are, -avi, -atum, vb. tr. *scatter, spread*, 11.

**diū**, diūtius, diūtissimē, advb. *for a long time*, 11.

**diūturnus**, -a, -um, adj. *lengthy, protracted*, 8.

**dīves**, -itis, adj. and noun, *rich, rich man*, 15.

**dīvido**, -ere, -vīsi, -vīsum, vb. tr. *divide up, apportion*, 7.

**dīvīnus**, -a, -um, adj. *divine, godlike*, 6.

**dīvitiae**, -arum, noun fem. plur. *riches, wealth*, 4.

**do**, dare, dedi, datum, vb. tr. *give*, 7.

**doleo**, dolere, dolui, vb. intr. *grieve*, 1.

dolor, -oris, noun masc. *grief*, 13.

dolus, -i, noun masc. *trick*, 6.

domesticus, -a, -um, adj. *domestic, private*, 20.

domicilium, -i, noun neut. *home, house*, 4.

dominus, -i, noun masc. *master*, 8.

domus, -us, noun fem. *house, household, family*, 4; do-mum, domos, *to...home*, 8; domi, locative, *at home*, 14; domo, *from home*, 12.

dōnec, conj. *until, until at last*, 4.

dōno, -are, -avi, -atum, vb. tr. *present*, 16.

dōnum, -i, noun neut. *gift*, 9.

dormio, -ire, -ivi, -itum, vb. intr. *sleep*, 5.

dubius, -a, -um, adj. *doubt-ful*, 5. The neuter is used as a noun, *doubt*, 5.

dūco, -ere, duxi, ductum, vb. tr. *lead*, 9; **in matrimon-ium** ducere, *marry*, 3. Used intransitively in 24 (**via duxit**). In 5 **cloacis ductis** trans. by *laid* (lit. *drawn*).

dum, subordinating conj. *while*, 1. (Other important uses are not illustrated in this book.)

duo, duae, duo, adj. *two*, 1.

duodēquadrāgēsimus, -a, -um, adj. *thirty-eighth*, 5.

dux, ducis, noun common, *leader, guide*, 6.

ēdīco, -ere, -dixi, edictum, vb. tr. *proclaim*, 15.

ēditus, -a, -um, *raised, ele-vated*, 24.

ēdo, -ere, -didi, -ditum, vb. tr. *give out, publish*, 4.

ēduco, -are, -avi, -atum, vb. tr. *bring up*, 5.

ēdūco, -ere, -duxi, -ductum, vb. tr. *lead out*, 20.

effero, -ferre, extuli, ēlātum, vb. tr. *uplift, exalt*, 4: *lift up*, 6: *carry out*, 10.

efficio, -ere, -fēci, -fectum, vb. tr. *bring about*, 21.

effigies, effigiei, noun fem. *image, symbol*, 9.

effūsē, advb. *widely*, 16.

effūsus, -a, -um (perf. part. of **effundo**), *spread out, wild*, 24.

egeo, -ere, egui, vb. intr. *be in want*, 13.

ego, pron. *I*, 1.

ēgredior, -i, -gressus, vb. intr. *go out*, 24.

ēicio, -ere, -iēci, -iectum, vb. tr. *drive out*, 11.

ēlābor, -i, -lapsus, vb. intr. *glide out*, 9.

ēligo, -ere, -lēgi, -lectum, vb. tr. *choose out*, 17.

ēmineo, -ere, -ui, vb. intr. *be conspicuous*, 13.

ēn, interjection, *behold*, 13.

enim, coordinating conj. *for*, 1.

eo, ire, ii, itum, vb. intr. *go*. With **obviam**, *go to meet*, 13.

eō, advb. *thither, to that place*, 10.

eques, -itis, noun masc. *horse-soldier*, 13.

equester, -tris, -tre, adj. *equestrian*, 17.

equus, -i, noun masc. *horse*, 13.

ergā, prep. followed by acous. *towards* (of friendly feelings), 4.

ergō, advb. *therefore*, 14.

ērigo, -ere, -rexi, -rectum, vb. tr. *uplift, rouse*, 6.

ēripio, -ere, -rïpui, -reptum, vb. tr. *snatch away from, deprive of*, 19.

erro, -are, -avi, -atum, vb. intr. *make a mistake, err*, 12.

error, -oris, noun masc. *mistake*, 18.

ērudio, -ire, -ivï, -itum, vb. tr. *train up*, 5.

ērumpo, -ere, -rūpi, -ruptum, vb. intr. *burst out, sally forth*, 21.

ēscendo, -ere, -ndi, -nsum, vb. intr. *climb up*, 14.

et, conj. *and*, 1: *also*, 19; et... et, *both...and*, 3.

etiam, advb. *also*, 4: *even*, 2.

ēvādo, -ere, -vāsi, -vāsum, vb. intr. *make one's way out*, 24.

ēveho, -ere, -vexi, -vectum, vb. tr. *carry off*, 5.

ēventus, -us, noun masc. *issue*, 2.

ex, prep. followed by abl. *out of*, 8, 9: *from*; agros ex hostibus captos, 7: ex eo loco, 2: ex planis locis, 5: ex aquila, 4: ex praeda, 9: ex superiore parte aedium, 6: *of*, ex quibus, 2: *since*, ex quo (anno), 5: *in accordance with*, ex foedere, 17: cf. 21: pendere ex, *hang upon*, 2; ex industria, *of set purpose*, 9.

exactus, -a, -um, adj. *advanced*, 14.

excēdo, -ere, -cessï, -cessum, vb. intr. *go out from, retire from*, 19.

excelsus, -a, -um, adj. *lofty*, 4.

excio, -cire, -civi, -citum, vb. tr. *call forth, arouse*, 5.

excipio, -ere, -cēpi, -ceptum, vb. tr. *take up, catch*, 6: *overhear*, 12: *receive, sustain*, 15.

excito, -are, -avi, -atum, vb. tr. *call forth, arouse*, 7.

exeo, -ire, -ii, -itum, vb. intr. *go out*, 21.

exercitus, -us, noun masc. *army*, 2.

exhibeo, -ere, -ui, -itum, vb. tr. *show, prove*, 4.

exigo, -ere, -ēgi, -actum, vb. tr. *drive out*, 14: *claim*, 11.

exiguus, -a, -um, adj. *small*, 15.

exitium, -i, noun neut. *death, destruction*, 8.

exonero, -are, -avi, -atum, vb. tr. *free from*, 11.

expello, -ere, -puli, -pulsum, vb. tr. *drive out, banish*, 11.

expers, -pertis, adj. *devoid of* (lit. *without a share in*), 2.

explōro, -are, -avi, -atum, vb. intr. *reconnoitre*, 13.

expugno, -are, -avi, -atum, vb. tr. *take by storm*, 16.

exsequor, -sequi, -secūtus, vb. tr. *carry out, fulfil*, 6: *harry*, 10.

exsilium, -i, noun neut. *exile*, 6.

exspecto, -are, -avi, -atum, vb. tr. *wait for*, 12.

exspiro, -are, -avi, -atum, vb. intr. *die*, 2.

**exsul**, -sulis, noun common, *exile*, 10.

**exsulo**, -are, -avi, -atum, vb. intr. *live in exile*, 10.

**exsulto**, -are, -avi, -atum, vb. intr. *exult, rejoice exceedingly*, 2.

**extemplō**, advb. *immediately, forthwith*, 7.

**exterreo**, -ere, -ui, -itum, vb. tr. *frighten*, 24.

**extorris**, -e, adj. *exiled*, 13.

**extrā**, prep. followed by accus. *outside*, 16.

**extraho**, -ere, -traxi, -tractum, vb. tr. *draw forth*, 10.

**extrēmus**, -a, -um, superlative of compar. adj. **exterior**, *utmost, extreme*, 21.

**exuo**, -ere, -ui, -ūtum, vb. tr. *despoil of, rob of* (with accus. of person and abl. of the thing), 20.

**fābula**, -ae, noun fem. *story*, 1.

**facile**, -ilius, -illimē, advb. *easily*, 1.

**facilis**, -e, adj. *easy*, 5.

**facinus**, -oris, noun neut. *deed, crime*, 6: *achievement*, 16.

**facio**, -ere, fēci, factum, vb. tr. *do, commit*, 6: *conduct* (**funus**), 13: *make*, 10; passive **fio**, 2.

**factum**, -i, noun neut. *deed*, 15.

**fallo**, -ere, fefelli, falsum, vb. tr. *disappoint*, 21.

**falsus**, -a, -um, adj. *false*, 4.

**fāma**, -ae, noun fem. *fame, rumour*, 4.

**fames**, -is, noun fem. *hunger, famine*, 21.

**familia**, -ae, noun fem. *family*, 24.

**familiāris**, -e, adj. and noun, *member of the household*, 5: *friend*, 22: *private*, 18: *belonging to the family*, 24.

**fascis**, -is, noun masc. Used in plur. to denote the bundle consisting of rods and an axe which was carried before the highest magistrates, 14.

**fastīgium**, -i, noun neut. *slope*, 5.

**fateor**, -eri, fassus, vb. tr. *admit*, 11.

**faustus**, -a, -um, adj. *lucky, successful*, 24.

**faveo**, -ere, fāvi, fautum, vb. intr. *favour, support*, governing dative, 8.

**favor**, -oris, noun masc. *support*, 14: *enthusiasm*, 24.

**fēlix**, -icis, adj. *successful*, 24.

**fēmina**, -ae, noun fem. *woman*, 6.

**fenestra**, -ae, noun fem. *window*, 6.

**ferē**, advb. *almost*, 16.

**ferio**, -ire, percussi, percussum, or ici, ictum, vb. tr. *strike*, 13: with **foedus**, *make*, 21.

**fero**, ferre, tuli, lātum, vb. tr. *bring*, 9: *propose* (a law), 14: *bear, endure*, 15; *bear on*, 24: with **aegerrime**, *resent*, 8: **ferunt**, *men say*, 5: **fertur**, (*it*) *is said*, 19: **osculum ferre**, *give a kiss*, 9.

**ferōciter**, ferōcius, ferōcissimē, advb. *boldly*, 7: *vehemently*, 8.

**ferox**, -ōcis, adj. *bold, spirited, warlike*, 2.

**ferrum**, -i, noun neut. *steel, sword*, 5.

**fessus**, -a, -um, adj. *weary*, 2.

**festīno**, -are, -avi, -atum, vb. intr. *hasten, hurry*, 10.

**fidēlis**, -e, adj. *faithful, trustworthy*, 10.

**fides**, fidei, noun fem. *good faith*, 12: *belief* (illa fides), 1; **fidem praestare**, *keep one's word*, 17.

**fidūcia**, -ae, noun fem. *confidence*, 14.

**fidus**, -a, -um, adj. *trustworthy*; with **pax**, *permanent*, 18.

**filia**, -ae, noun fem. *daughter*, 3.

**filius**, -i, noun masc. *son*, 3.

**finio**, -ire, -ivi, -itum, vb. tr. *bring to an end*, 18: *confine*, v.

**finis**, -is, noun masc. *end, limit*, 16.

**finitimus**, -a, -um, adj. *neighbouring*, 3.

**fio**, fieri, factus, vb. intr. *be done* or *made*, 20; *take place*, 1.

**firmo**, -are, -avi, -atum, vb. tr. *strengthen*, 6.

**flagro**, -are, -avi, -atum, vb. intr. *be in a blaze*, 20.

**flamma**, -ae, noun fem. *flame, blaze*, 5.

**flecto**, -ere, flexi, flexum, vb. tr. *bend, sway*, 20.

**flētus**, -us, noun masc. *weeping*, 22.

**flūmen**, -inis, noun neuter, *river, stream*, 15.

**foedus**, -eris, noun neuter, *treaty*, 8.

**forās**, advb. *out of doors*, 6.

**forte**, advb. *as it happened*, 2.

**fortis**, -e, adj. *brave*, 4.

**fortūna**, -ae, noun fem. *fortune, good fortune*, 1. In plur. *goods, property*, 4.

**forum**, -i, noun neuter, *market-place, forum*, 5.

**fossa**, -ae, noun fem. *trench*, 20.

**fragor**, -oris, noun masc. *crash*, 1.

**frango**, -ere, frēgi, fractum, vb. tr. *break, crush*, 20.

**frāter**, -tris, noun masc. *brother*, 2.

**fraus**, fraudis, noun fem. *treachery*, 5.

**frequens**, -entis, adj. *crowded*. In plur. *in large numbers*, 8.

**frētus**, -a, -um, adj. *used with abl. relying on*, 23.

**frūmentum**, -i, noun neuter, *corn*, 15. In plur. *standing crops*, 21.

**frustrā**, advb. *in vain, to no purpose*, 20.

**frustror**, -ari, -atus, vb. tr. *baffle, elude*, 17: *deceive*, 18.

**fuga**, -ae, noun fem. *flight*, 2.

**fugio**, -ere, fūgi, fut. part. fugiturus, vb. intr. *flee*, 6.

**fugo**, -are, -avi, -atum, vb. tr. *put to flight*, 13.

**fulgeo**, -ere, fulsi, vb. intr. *shine, glitter*, 2.

**fundāmentum**, -i, noun neuter, *foundation*, 9.

**fundo**, -ere, fūdi, fūsum, vb. tr. *rout*, 13.

**fūnus**, -eris, noun neuter, *funeral*, 18.

**gaudium**, -i, noun neuter, *joy*, 15.

**gener**, -eri, noun masc. *son-in-law*, 5.

**gens**, gentis, noun fem. *race, clan*, 10. Plur. *nations*, 12.

**genus**, -eris, noun neuter, *race*, 11, 15: *kind*, 17.

**gero**, -ere, gessi, gestum, vb. tr. *wage* (with **bellum**), 2: *do*, 14: *cherish* (with **animum** or **animos**), 16, 21; **rem bene gerere**, *succeed*, 20.

**gigno**, -ere, genui, genitum, vb. tr. *beget*, 3.

**gladius**, -i, noun masc. *sword*, 2.

**glisco**, -ere, vb. intr. *grow, come on*, 19.

**glŏria**, -ae, noun fem. *fame, glory*, 14.

**gradus**, -us, noun masc. *step*, 7: *stride*, 15.

**grātia**, -ae, noun fem. *favour*; **in gratiam reconciliare**, *reconcile*, 8: plur. *thanks*, 24.

**grātuītus**, -a, -um, adj. *unrewarded*, 7.

**grātus**, -a, -um, adj. *pleasing, acceptable*, 14.

**gravis**, -e, adj. *heavy, weighty, important*, 1: *obstinately contested* (with **proelium**), 19.

**habeo**, -ere, -ui, -itum, vb. tr. *have, hold*, 7; **curam habere**, *have regard for, pay attention to*, 15: **in animo habere**, *have in mind*, 4: **comitia habere**, *hold election*, 14: **sermonem habere**, *have a conversation*,

7: **orationem habere**, *deliver a speech*, 4; *regard as*, 5; **pro certo**, 5: **pro transfuga**, 16: **pro hoste**, 19.

**habito**, -are, -avi, -atum, vb. intr. *live, dwell*, 10.

**haereo**, -ere, haesi, haesum, vb. intr. *stick fast*, 15.

**hasta**, -ae, noun fem. *spear*, 19.

**haud**, advb. *not*, 4.

**hērēs**, hērēdis, noun common, *heir*, 4.

**hesternus**, -a, -um, adj. *belonging to yesterday, of yesterday*, 8.

**hic**, adj. and pron. *this, this man*, 1.

**hīc**, advb. *here*, 23.

**hinc**, advb. *from here*, 8: *from this source*, 11; **hinc... hinc**, *on the one side...on the other side*, 1.

**hodiē**, advb. *to-day*, 1.

**homo**, -inis, noun common, *human being, person, man*, 1.

**honor**, -oris, noun masc. *honour*, 5.

**honŏro**, -are, -avi, -atum, vb. tr. *honour*, 17.

**hŏra**, -ae, noun fem. *hour*, 12.

**horror**, -oris, noun masc. *shudder, thrill*, 2.

**hospitium**, -i, noun neut. *hospitality*, 21.

**hostīlis**, -e, adj. *belonging to an enemy, of an enemy*, 21.

**hostis**, gen. hostis, noun common, *enemy, opponent*, 2.

**hūiusmodī**, adj. indeclinable, *of this kind, such*, 16.

**hūmānus**, -a, -um, adj. *human*, 19.

**humilis, -e,** humilior, humillimus, adj. *lowly,* 4.

**iaceo,** -ere, -ui, vb. intr. *lie,* 2.
**iacio,** -ere, iēci, iactum, vb. tr. *throw, utter,* 16.
**iam,** advb. *already,* 2: *now,* 12.
**iamdūdum,** advb. *for a long time already,* 7.
**ibi,** advb. *there,* 3.
**ictus,** -us, noun masc. *blow,* 6.
**ictus,** -a, -um, perf. ptc. of ferio, *strike,* 23; **foedus ictum est,** *a treaty was made,* 21.
**īdem, eadem, idem,** adj. and pron. *the same,* 15.
**igitur,** advb. *therefore,* 2.
**ignārus,** -a, -um, adj. *ignorant,* 16.
**ignāvus,** -a, -um, adj. *cowardly,* 7.
**ignis,** -is, noun masc. *fire,* 6.
**ignōro,** -are, -avi, -atum, vb. tr. *not to know, be ignorant of,* 16.
**ille, illa, illud,** adj. and pron. *that, that man,* 1.
**illīc,** advb. *there,* 24.
**imāgo,** -inis, noun fem. *likeness, bust,* 7.
**immātūrus,** -a, -um, adj. *unripe, premature,* 22.
**immineo,** -ere, -ui, vb. intr. *be imminent, threaten,* 12: *overhang, be adjacent to,* 21.
**imminuo,** -ere, -ui, -ūtum, vb. tr. *diminish,* 8.
**immortālitas,** -atis, noun fem. *immortality,* 1.
**impello,** -ere, -puli, -pulsum, vb. tr. *drive, induce,* 21. In passive, *receive a shock,* 19.

**imperātor,** -oris, noun masc. *commander-in-chief,* 19.
**imperium,** -i, noun neut. *supreme command,* 2: *empire,* 9: *authority,* 10.
**impero,** -are, -avi, -atum, vb. intr. *command, rule,* 15.
**impetro,** -are, -avi, -atum, vb. trans. *gain a request,* 23.
**impetus,** -us, noun masc. *violence, charge, attack,* 2, 15.
**impleo,** -plere, -plevi, -pletum, vb. tr. *fill,* 9.
**imprōvidus,** -a, -um, adj. *not foreseeing, reckless,* 24.
**impūbis,** -e, adj. *youthful, young,* 17.
**īmus,** -a, -um, superlative adj., comparative nferior, *lowest*; **imus clivus,** *the bottom of the slope* or *hill,* 14.
**in,** prep. with accus. *into,* 1: *on to,* 6: *against,* 2: *towards,* 4, 16: *upon,* **intentus in,** 21: *for,* **in diem certam,** 8: **in dies,** *day by day,* 7: **in perpetuum,** *for ever, in perpetuity,* 18. With abl. *in,* 1: *on,* 5: *among,* **in primis,** 15.
**incautus,** -a, -um, adj. *incautious, reckless,* 23.
**incēdo,** -ere, -cessi, -cessum, vb. tr. and intr. *march along,* 13: *come upon,* 18.
**incendo,** -ere, -cendi, -censum, vb. tr. *kindle, fire, rouse,* 8.
**incertus,** -a, -um, adj. *uncertain, doubtful,* 3.
**inchoo,** -are, -avi, -atum, vb. tr. *begin,* 5.
**incido,** -ere, -i, vb. intr. *fall upon,* 24: **incido in,** *fall in*

*with*, 23: *turn up*, 24: *happen*, 10.

**incīdo**, -ere, -cīdi, -cīsum, vb. tr. *cut into, cut off*, 18.

**incipio**, -ere, -cēpi, -ceptum, vb. tr., 11; but see **coepi**.

**incito**, -are, -avi, -atum, vb. tr. *rouse, work upon*, 4.

**inclīno**, -are, -avi, -atum, vb. tr. and intr. *bend, give way*, 19, 24; **rem inclinatam**, *the failing fortunes* (of the fight), 23.

**inclūdo**, -ere, -clūsi, -clūsum, vb. tr. *shut up in*, 9.

**incolumis**, -e, adj. *safe, unhurt*, 15.

**increpo**, -are, -ui, -itum, vb. tr. and intr. *clash*, 2; **multa increpo in**, *inveigh at length against*, 8.

**incultus**, -a, -um, adj. *uncultivated*, 21.

**inde**, advb. *after this, then, thence*, 5, 9, 13.

**indīco**, -ere, -indixi, indictum, vb. tr. *appoint, proclaim*; **diem concilii**, 8: **bellum** 9: **exsilium**, 10.

**indictus**, -a, -um, adj. *unsaid, unheard*; **indictā causā**, *without pleading his cause*, 8.

**indignitas**, -atis, noun fem. *disgrace*, 21.

**indignus**, -a, -um, adj. *undeserved, cruel*, 7.

**indūco**, -ere, -duxi, -ductum, vb. tr. *lead into*, 7; **in animum inducere**, *make up one's mind to*, 18, *conceive the idea of*, 13.

**indulgentia**, -ae, noun fem. *indulgence, kindliness*, 5.

**induo**, -ere, -ui, -ūtum, vb. tr. *put on, assume*, 9.

**(ex) industriā**, prepositional phrase, *of set purpose, deliberately*, 9.

**ineo**, -ire, -ii, -itum, vb. tr. *enter*, 19: *enter into* (**amicitiam**), 20.

**inermis**, -e, adj. *unarmed*, 20.

**iners**, gen. -ertis, adj. *idle, useless*, 10.

**inexōrābilis**, -c, adj. *inexorable*, 12.

**inexpugnābilis**, -e, adj. *impregnable*, 14.

**infēlīciter**, advb. *unsuccessfully, without success*, 21.

**infēlix**, -icis, adj. *ill-omened*, 24.

**infensus**, -a, -um, adj. *embittered*, 16.

**inferi**, -orum, noun masc. plur. *those below, the world below*, 2.

**inferior**, -ius, gen. inferioris, comparative adj. *lower*, 7.

**infero**, -ferre, -tuli, -lātum, vb. tr. *carry in*, 8: *bring against*; **iniuriam inferre**, *offer an insult to*, 10: **bellum inferre**, *make war upon*, 20.

**infestus**, -a, -um, adj. used in active and passive senses, *hostile, dangerous*, 13: *exposed to attack*, 7: **infestis armis**, *with weapons pointed against one another*, 13.

**infidēlis**, -e, adj. *faithless*, 4.

**infimus**, -a, -um, adj. superlative, alternative to **imus**, *lowest*, 5.

**inflammo**, -are, -avi, -atum, vb. tr. *inflame*, 13.

**infrā**, preposition foll. by accusative, *below*, 14.

**ingenium**, -i, noun neut. *character, disposition*, 3.

**ingens**, -entis, adj. *great, huge*, 2.

**ingrātus**, -a, -um, adj. *ungrateful*, 13.

**ingredior**, -gredi, -gressus, vb. tr. *enter*, 4.

**inicio**, -ere, -iēci, -iectum, vb. tr. *throw upon, thrust into*, 8, 16.

**inimīcus**, -a, -um, adj. *hostile*, 21.

**iniūrātus**, -a, -um, adj. *without having taken an oath, unsworn*, 23.

**iniūria**, -ae, noun fem. *wrong, insult*, 10.

**inlūcescit**, inluxit, vb. intr. *it grows light*, 13.

**innocens**, -entis, adj. *guiltless*, 8.

**innūbo**, -ere, -nupsi, -nuptum, vb. intr. *marry into* (with **in** and acc.), 4.

**inopia**, -ae, noun fem. *scarcity*, 16.

**inops**, -opis, adj. *poor, helpless*, 12.

**inquit**, vb. parenthetical, *said he*, 1.

**inquiunt**, vb. parenthetical, *said they*, 9.

**inritus**, -a, -um, adj. *ineffectual*; ad inritum cadere, *prove ineffectual, be baffled*, 13.

**inrumpo**, -ere, -rūpi, -ruptum, vb. intr. *burst in*, 7.

**inruptio**, -onis, noun fem. *inrush, incursion*, 23.

**insequor**, -i, -secūtus, vb. tr. and intr. *follow*, 23.

**insideo**, -ere, -sēdi, -sessum, vb. intr. *be seated on*, 17.

**insidiae**, -arum, noun fem. plur. *ambush, plot*, 5.

**insignia**, -ium, noun neut. plur. *trappings of office, insignia*, 13.

**insignis**, -e, adj. *notable, noteworthy, distinguished*, 13.

**inspicio**, -ere, -spexi, -spectum, vb. tr. *inspect, look at*, 6.

**instituo**, -ere, -ui, -ūtum, vb. tr. *appoint*, 4.

**instruo**, -ere, -struxi, -structum, vb. tr. *draw up, marshal*, 19, 24.

**intactus**, -a, -um, adj. *untouched*, 16.

**integer**, -gra, -grum, adj. *whole, unhurt*, 2.

**intellego**, -ere, -lexi, -lectum, vb. tr. *realize, understand*, 3.

**intentus**, -a, -um, adj. *intent, eager*, 6 : *ready*, 18.

**inter**, prep. foll. by accus. *between*, 2 : *among, amid*, 3, 9 : *during*, 13.

**interdiū**, advb. *by day*, 7.

**intereā**, advb. *meanwhile*, 13.

**intereo**, -ire, -ii, -itum, vb. intr. *perish*, 20.

**interficio**, -ere, -fēci, -fectum, vb. tr. *kill*, 2.

**interiaceo**, -ere, -ui, vb. intr. *lie between*, 24.

**interim**, advb. *meanwhile*, 6.

**interregnum**, -i, noun neut. *interregnum*, 3.

**interrogo**, -are, -avi, -atum, vb. tr. *question*, 17.

FL 6

interrumpo, -ere, -rūpi, -ruptum, vb. tr. *break down*, 15.

intervallum, -i, noun neut. *interval, distance between*, 2.

intervenio, -ire, -vēni, -ventum, vb. intr. *interrupt* (with dative), 7: *intervene*, 20.

intestīnus, -a, -um, adj. *internal*, 20.

intrā, prep. followed by accus. *within*, of place and time, 14, 16.

intro, -are, -avi, -atum, vb. intr. *enter*, 16.

intus, advb. *within*, 21.

invādo, -ere, -vāsi, -vāsum, vb. tr. *assail*, 15: *invade*, 20.

invalidus, -a, -um, adj. *weak, enfeebled*, 14.

invehor, invehi, invectus, passive of inveho used as deponent; *ride on*, 19: invehor in, *inveigh against*, 8.

invenio, -ire, -vēni, -ventum, vb. tr. *find, discover*, 10.

invicem, advb. *in turn*, 6.

invictus, -a, -um, adj. *invincible*, 24.

invidia, -ae, noun fem. *envy, ill-will*, 14.

inviolātus, -a, -um, adj. *unharmed, uninjured*, 16.

invīsus, -a, -um, adj. *hateful*, 11.

invīto, -are, -avi, -atum, vb. tr. *invite, entertain*, 12.

ipse, -a, -um, emphasizing adj. *myself, yourself, himself*, 4.

īra, -ae, noun fem. *anger, wrath*, 8.

is, ea, id, adj. and pron. *that, he*, 1.

iste, ista, istud, adj. *that of yours*, 16.

ita, adv. *thus*, 1.

itaque, advb. *consequently, therefore*, 3.

iter, itineris, noun neut. *way, route*, 15.

iterum, advb. *a second time, again*, 21.

iubeo, -ere, iussi, iussum, vb. tr. *bid, order*, 4.

iugum, -i, noun neut. *mountain-ridge*, 20.

iungo, -ere, iunxi, iunctum, vb. tr. *join, unite*, 7.

iūro, -are, -avi, -atum, vb. tr. *swear*, 10.

iūs, iūris, noun neut. *law, right*, 4, 21; iura reddere, *administer justice*, 6.

iuvenis, -is, noun masc. *young man*, 5.

iuventus, -utis, noun fem. *youth, young men*, 12.

labor, -oris, noun masc. *labour, toil*, 10.

lābor, lābi, lapsus, vb. intr. *slip down*, 13.

lacesso, -ere, -ivi, -itum, vb. tr. *provoke, molest*, 20.

lacrima, -ae, noun fem. *tear*, 22.

lacus, -us, noun masc. *lake*, 19.

laedo, -ere, laesi, laesum, vb. tr. *injure, harm*, 10.

laetus, -a, -um, adj. *cheerful, good* (of augurium), 4.

lapicīda, -ae, noun masc. *stonemason*, 10.

latus, -eris, noun neut. *side*, 19.

laudo, -are, -avi, -atum, vb. tr. *praise, commend,* 14.

laus, laudis, noun fem. *praise, eulogy,* 21.

lēgātus, -i, noun masc. *ambassador,* 12: *officer,* 19.

legio, -onis, noun fem. *body of troops*: in plur. *troops,* 13.

lego, legere, lēgi, lectum, vb. tr. *pick up, collect,* 13: *choose,* 21.

lēnio, -ire, -ivi, -itum, vb. tr. *soothe,* 15.

lēniter, advb. *gently,* 24.

lex, lēgis, noun fem. *law, legal enactment,* 12.

liber, -bri, noun masc. *book,* 1.

līber, -era, -erum, adj. *free,* 18.

līberālis, -e, adj. *befitting a free man, liberal, noble,* 5.

līberātor, -oris, noun masc. *deliverer,* 10.

līberi, -orum, noun masc. plur. *children* (used of children in relation to their parents), 4.

lībero, -are, -avi, -atum, vb. tr. *set free,* 13.

lībertas, -atis, noun fem. *freedom,* 11.

licet, infin. licere, vb. impersonal, *it is permissible,* 15.

lictor, -oris, noun masc. *magistrate's attendant, lictor,* 6.

ligneus, -a, -um, adj. *made of wood,* 9.

līmen, -inis, noun neuter, *threshold,* 24.

litterae, -arum, noun fem. plur. *letter, epistle,* 12.

loco, -are, -avi, -atum, vb. tr. *post, station,* 16.

locus, loci, plur. loca, 5: noun masc. in sing., neut. in plur. *scope,* 4: *place,* 2: *situation, position,* 4.

longē, advb. *far,* 8: *by far* (longe princeps), 21.

longus, -a, -um, adj. *long,* 16.

loquor, loqui, locūtus, vb. tr. and intr. *say, speak,* 1.

luctus, -us, noun masc. *grief,* 10.

lūcus, -i, noun masc. *grove,* 8.

lūgeo, -ere, luxi, vb. tr. *mourn for,* 13.

lūmen, -inis, noun neut. *light,* 5.

lux, lūcis, noun fem. *light*; primā luce, *at dawn,* 1.

māchinor, -ari, -atus, vb. tr. *contrive, plot,* 8.

maestitia, -ae, noun fem. *sadness, gloom,* 2.

maestus, -a, -um, adj. *melancholy, dejected,* 10.

magis, advb., comparative of magnopere, *more,* 21.

magister, -tri, noun masc. *master, teacher,* 4; magister equitum, *chief of the cavalry, master of the horse,* 19.

magistrātus, -us, noun masc. *office, magistracy,* 14: *magistrate,* 20.

magnificē, -entius, -entissimē, adv. *splendidly,* 13.

magnus, -a, -um, māior, maximus, advb. *great, loud,* 1.

māiestas, -atis, noun fem. *majesty, dignity,* 14.

**māior**, māius, gen. māiōris, comparative adj. *greater, elder*, 7, 13.

**malus**, -a, -um, pēior, pessimus, adj. *bad, evil*, 15.

**mandātum**, -i, noun neut., plur. *instructions*, 9.

**maneo**, -ere, -si, -sum, vb. tr. and intr. *remain*, 11: *wait*, 20: *await*, 22.

**manifestus**, -a, -um, adj. *clear*, 5.

**manipulus**, -i, noun masc. *company of soldiers*, 19.

**māno**, -are, -avi, -atum, vb. intr. *flow, spread*, 24.

**manus**, -us, noun fem. *hand*, 16; manus conserere, *join battle, engage in combat*, 2: *band* (of soldiers), 21.

**marītus**, -i, noun masc. *husband*, 7.

**Mars**, Martis, noun masc.; Marte incerto, *with doubtful success*, 8. See vocab. of proper names.

**māter**, -tris, noun fem. *mother*, 9.

**māteria**, -ae, noun fem. *timber*, 14.

**mātrimōnium**, -i, noun neut. *marriage*, 3.

**mātrōna**, -ae, noun fem. *married woman, matron*, 13.

**mātūro**, -are, -avi, -atum, vb. tr. *hasten, expedite*, 20.

**mātūrus**, -a, -um, adj. *ripe*, 14.

**maximē**, advb., superlative to magnopere, *chiefly, especially*, 13.

**maximus**, -a, -um, adj., superlative to magnus, *greatest*, 1.

**mēcum**, abl. of ego followed by cum, *with me*, 8.

**medium**, -i, noun neut. *the middle, the midst*, 1.

**medius**, -a, -um, adj. *in the middle*, 7: *between the two*, 3: *the middle of*, 1.

**melior**, -us, adj., comparative to bonus, *better*, 12.

**membrum**, -i, noun neut. *member, limb*, 20.

**memini**, -isse, perf. tense of a defective vb. used with pres. meaning, *remember*, 11.

**memor**, memoris, adj. used with gen. case, *mindful*, 13.

**mens**, mentis, noun fem. *mind*; plur. *feelings*, 20.

**mentio**, -onis, noun fem. *mention*, 12.

**metus**, -us, noun masc. *fear*, 8.

**meus**, -a, -um, possessive adj. *my*, 7.

**mico**, -are, micui, vb. intr. *flash*, 2.

**migro**, -are, -avi, -atum, vb. intr. *migrate, be off to*, 4.

**miles**, -itis, noun masc. *soldier*, 16.

**mīlitia**, -ae, noun fem. *military service*, 1; militiae, loc. *on service abroad*, 14.

**mīlito**, -are, -avi, -atum, vb. intr. *serve as a soldier*, 20.

**mille**, numeral adj. in sing.: plural millia used as a neuter noun, *thousand*, 3.

**mina**, -ae, noun fem. *threat*, 16.

**minimus**, -a, -um, adj., superlative to parvus, *smallest, youngest*, 10.

**minister**, -tri, noun masc. *attendant, servant*, 6.

**ministērium**, -i, noun neut. *service, duty*, 13.

**minitor**, -ari, -atus, vb. tr. and intr. *threaten*, 21, 24.

**minor**, minus, adj., comparative to **parvus**, *smaller, younger*, 7.

**minus**, advb., comparative to **parum**, 11.

**mīrābilis**, -e, adj. *wonderful, remarkable*, 1.

**mīrāculum**, -i, noun neuter, *marvel, miracle*, 15.

**mīrus**, -a, -um, adj. *wonderful*, 8.

**miser**, -a, -um, **miserior**, **miserrimus**, adj. *wretched*, 22.

**miseria**, -ae, noun fem. *misery, wretchedness*, 10.

**miseror**, -ari, -atus, vb. tr. *express pity for*, 13.

**mitto**, -ere, mīsi, missum, vb. tr. *send*, 7.

**modo**, advb. *only*, 14.

**modus**, -i, noun masc. *way, manner*, 19.

**moenia**, moenium, noun neut. plur. *walls*, 22.

**mōlior**, -iri, -itus, vb. tr. *work at, set about*, 12.

**moneo**, -ere, -ui, -itum, vb. tr. *advise, recommend*, 10.

**mons**, montis, noun masc. *mountain, hill*, 9.

**monumentum**,-i,noun neut. *monument, memorial*, 9.

**mora**, -ae, noun fem. *delay*, 8.

**moribundus**, -a, -um, adj. *in a dying condition*, 10.

**morior**, mori, mortuus, vb. intr. *die*, 3.

**moror**, -ari, -atus, vb. intr. *delay*, 8.

**mors**, -tis, noun fem. *death*, 1.

**mortāles**, -ium, plur. of adj. **mortalis** used as noun, *subject to death, living creature*, 9.

**mortifer**, -fera, -ferum, adj. *deadly, fatal*, 23.

**mōs**, mōris, noun masc. *custom*, 3: *style*, 12.

**moveo**, -ere, mōvi, mōtum, vb. tr. *move, influence*, 10: *move forward, carry forward*, 23.

**mox**, advb. *soon*, 2.

**muliebris**, -e, adj. *womanish*, 22.

**mulier**, mulieris, noun fem. *woman*, 7.

**multi**, -ae, -a, plur. adj. *many*, 1.

**multitūdo**, -inis, noun fem. *multitude, number*, 3.

**multo**, abl. of the noun **multum**, used to qualify a comparative, etc., 13, 18.

**multum**, noun of quantity and advb. *much*, 9.

**mūnificē**, -entius, -entissimē, advb. *munificently, bountifully*, 11.

**mūnio**, -ire, -ivi, -itum, vb. tr. *fortify*, 14.

**mūnus**, -eris, noun neut. *duty, function*, 6.

**mūrus**, -i, noun masc. *wall*, 15.

**mūtābilis**, -e, adj. *changeable, fickle*, 14.

**nam**, conjunction, *for*, 7.

**narro**, -are, -avi, -atum, vb. tr. *relate*, 1.

**nascor**, -i, nātus, vb. intr.

*be born*, **4.** Used with abl. in 7, =*born of.*

**nātus, -us,** noun masc. *birth, age,* 22.

**-ne,** interrogative word used in asking questions to which there is no obvious answer. It stands at the end of the first word in the sentence, 14.

**nē,** subordinating conjunction introducing negative clauses of purpose and desire, *in order that not: that not,* 7, 11. After vb. of fearing in 16, **veritus ne,** *fearing that.*

**nē...quidem,** advbs. *not... even,* 5. The word or words emphasized are placed between the **ne** and the **quidem.**

**nec** or **neque,** conjunction, *neither, and...not,* 1.

**nec...nec,** *neither...nor,* 2.

**necesse est,** verb equivalent, *it is necessary,* 5.

**nego, -are, -avi, -atum,** vb. tr. *say that not,* 5.

**nēmō,** gen. nullius, pron. *no one,* 13.

**nepōs,** nepōtis, noun masc. *grandson,* 3.

**nēquāquam,** advb. *in no way,* 21.

**neque.** Cf. **nec.**

**nēquīquam,** advb. *in vain, to no purpose,* 15.

**nescio,** nescire, nescivi or nescii, vb. tr. *not to know,* 16.

**neuter, -tra, -trum,** gen. neutrius, adj. and pron. *neither,* 13.

**nēve,** conjunction, *and not.*

Used in clauses of purpose and dependent desire: e.g. 9, of purpose. Sometimes also in non-dependent desires, 24.

**nī.** Cf. **nisi,** 23.

**nihil,** indeclinable noun of quantity, *nothing,* 11; with integral genitive depending upon it, 19.

**nihilo,** abl. of **nihilum,** a parallel form to **nihil,** *by nothing, in no way*: used to qualify comparatives, 21.

**nihilōminus,** advb. *nevertheless, notwithstanding,* 15.

**nimbus, -i,** noun masc. *cloud,* 1.

**nimis,** advb. *excessively*; **nimis magnum pretium,** *too high a price,* 15.

**nisi,** sub.conj. *unless, if...not,* 20.

**nītor,** nīti, nīsus or nixus, vb. intr. *strive, struggle,* 24.

**nōbilis, -e,** adj. *of noble birth,* 12.

**noctū,** advb. *by night,* 7.

**nōlo,** nolle, nōlui, imperative noli, nolite, vb. tr. *be unwilling,* 7.

**nōmen, -inis,** noun neuter, *name,* 3.

**nōn,** advb. *not,* 2.

**nondum,** advb. *not yet,* 2.

**nonne,** interrogative word used to introduce a question to which the natural answer would be "yes," 22.

**nōs,** gen. nostrum (if the use is integral), pron. *we,* 9.

**noster,-tra,-trum,** adj. *our,* 5.

**novus, -a, -um,** adj. *new, fresh,* 3: *strange,* 11.

**nūbo**, -ere, nupsi, nuptum, vb. intr. *marry* (with the woman as subject), but perf. part. pass. in 7.

**nūdo**, -are, -avi, -atum, vb. tr. *strip*, 13.

**nullus**, -a, -um, gen. nullius, adj. *none at all*, 18; **nullo modo**, *in no way*, 19.

**num**, interrogative word used to introduce a non-dependent question to which the obvious answer would be "no," 22. Also used to introduce dependent questions, "whether," 17.

**numerus**, -i, noun masc. *number, quantity*, 8.

**nunc**, advb. *now*, 13.

**nunquam**, advb. *never*, 14.

**nuntio**, -are, -avi, -atum, vb. tr. *announce, report*, 1.

**nuntius**, -i, noun masc. *messenger, message*, 7.

**nuptiae**, -arum, noun fem. plur. *marriage*, 7.

**nurus**, -us, noun fem. *daughter-in-law*, 22.

**nūtrio**, -ire, -ivi, -itum, vb. tr. *nourish, bring up*, 5.

**ob**, prep. foll. by accus. *on account of*, 3.

**obeo**, -ire, -ii, -itum, vb. tr. *fulfil* (**munera**), 14; **mortem obire**, *die*, 14.

**obicio**, -ere, -iēci, -iectum, vb. tr. *fling against, expose to*, 2: *fling in the way of* (as a barrier), 15.

**obloquor**, -loqui, -locūtus, vb. intr. *speak against*, 6.

**obsaepio**, -ire, -saepsi, -saep-tum, vb. tr. *block, bar against*, 13.

**obsecro**, -are, -avi, -atum, vb. tr. *entreat, implore*, 11.

**obsequium**, -i, noun neuter, *complaisance, obliging ways*, 4.

**observantia**, -ae, noun fem. *attention, respect*, 4.

**observo**, -are, -avi, -atum, vb. tr. *keep, observe*; **diem observare**, *keep an appointment for a particular day*, 8.

**obses**, -sidis, noun common, *hostage*, 16.

**obsideo**, -ere, -sēdi, -sessum, vb. tr. *besiege*, 16.

**obsidio**, -onis, noun fem. *siege*, 10.

**obsisto**, -ere, obstiti, vb. intr. *stand in the way of*, 11.

**obstinātus**, -a, -um, adj. *settled, fixed, obstinate, inflexible*, 18, 22.

**obsto**, -are, -stiti, vb. intr. *stand in the way of, thwart, obstruct*, 11.

**obstrepo**, -ere, -ui, vb. intr. *cry against, make a noise against*, 6.

**obstupefacio**, -facere, -fēci, -factum, vb. tr. *astound*, 15.

**obtestor**, -ari, -atus, vb. tr. *appeal to*, 15.

**obtineo**, -ere, -ui, vb. tr. *hold*, 15.

**obtrunco**, -are, -avi, -atum, vb. tr. *cut down, kill*, 16.

**obtundo**, -ere, -tudi, -tūsum, vb. tr. *beat upon, annoy*, 18.

**obviam**, advb. *in the way of*; **obviam eo**, *go to meet*, 13:

**obviam ago,** *drive in the way of,* 24.

**occāsio,** -onis, noun fem. *opportunity,* 12.

**occāsus,** -us, noun masc. *setting* (of the sun), 8.

**occĭdo,** -ere, -cĭdi, -cīsum, vb. tr. *kill,* 2.

**occupo,** -are, -avi, -atum, vb. tr. *seize* (with **regnum**), **5**: pass. *be busy with,* 10.

**occurro,** -ere, -curri, -cursum, vb. intr. *meet,* 1.

**oculus,** -i, noun masc. *eye,* 13.

**odium,** -i, noun neuter, *hatred,* 13.

**offendo,** -ere, -ndi, -nsum, vb. tr. *strike against, offend,* 11.

**offero,** -ferre, obtuli, oblātum, vb. tr. *offer, present,* 28: *bring up against* (of a charge), 8.

**ōlim,** advb. *once upon a time,* 3: *one day* (in the future), 1.

**omnis,** omne, adj. sing. *whole,* 1: *every* (latus omne), v: plur. *all,* 1.

**onus,** -eris, noun neuter, *burden,* 15.

**opem,** opis, noun fem. without nom. sing. in this use, sing. *help,* 13: plur. *power, resources,* 6.

**operio,** -ire, -ui, opertum, vb. tr. *wrap, cover,* 1.

**opifex,** opificis, noun common, *workman,* 10.

**oportet,** -ere, impersonal vb. used with accus. and infin. *it behoves, must,* 14.

**oppidāni,** -orum, noun masc. plur. *townspeople,* 21.

**oppidum,** -i, noun neuter, *town,* 21.

**oppōno,** -ere, -posui, -positum, vb. tr. *set opposite, set to oppose,* 23.

**opportūnus,** -a, -um, adj. *suitable,* 24.

**opprimo,** -ere, -pressi, -pressum, vb. tr. *ruin, bring to ruin,* 8: *crush,* 12.

**oppugno,** -are, -avi, -atum, vb. tr. *attack,* 20.

**optimus,** -a, -um, adj., superlative to **bonus,** *best, excellent,* 4.

**opulentus,** -a, -um, adj. *rich, wealthy,* 24.

**opus,** operis, noun neuter, *work, achievement,* 1; **opus est,** with dat. of the person and abl. of the thing, *there is need of,* 18.

**ōrāculum,** -i, noun neuter, *oracle,* 9.

**ōrātio,** -onis, noun fem. *speech,* 4.

**orbis,** -is, noun masc. *circle*; **orbis terrarum,** *world,* 1.

**ordino,** -are, -avi, -atum, vb. tr. *put in order, arrange,* 18.

**ordo,** -dinis, noun masc. *line,* 16: plur. *ranks,* 15.

**orīgo,** -ginis, noun fem. *origin, birth,* 1.

**orior,** oriri, ortus, vb. intr. *arise,* 5; **ortus** with abl. *sprung from,* 3: *born,* 4.

**ornātus,** -us, noun masc. *dress, apparel,* 16.

**ōro,** -are, -avi, -atum, vb. tr. *entreat,* 10.

**ōs,** ōris, noun neuter, *mouth, face,* 20, 23.

osculum, -i, noun neuter, *kiss,* 9.

paene, advb. *almost,* 4.

pālor, -ari, -atus, vb. intr. *roam, straggle about,* 24.

palūdātus, -a, -um, adj. *wearing a general's cloak,* 24.

pālus, -i, noun masc. *stake,* 13.

pār, gen. paris, adj. *equal, alike,* 2.

parens, -entis, noun common, *parent,* 1.

pāreo, -ere, -ui, vb. intr. *obey,* 18.

parma, -ae, noun fem. *small, round shield,* 13.

paro, -are, -avi, -atum, vb. tr. *prepare,* 8; insidias parare, *lay a plot,* 5.

parricīdium, -i, noun neut. *murder,* 7.

pars, partis, noun fem. *part,* 6; ab eā parte, *on that side,* 19: in inferiorem partem, *down,* 7.

partim...partim, advb. *partly...partly,* 24.

parumper, advb. *for a short time,* 15.

parvus, -a, -um, adj. *small,* 14.

passim, advb. *in all directions,* 21.

pastor, -oris, noun masc. *shepherd,* 6.

patefacio, -ere, -fēci, -factum, vb. tr. *open, disclose,* 6.

pateo, -ere, -ui, vb. intr. *be open,* 21.

pater, -tris, noun masc. *father,* 3. In plur. *senators,* 7; *patricians,* 20.

paternus, -a, -um, adj. *belonging to a father,* 13.

patientia, -ae, noun fem *patience, forbearance,* 3.

patior, pati, passus, vb. tr *endure,* 21: *suffer,* 22: *permit,* 7.

patria, -ae, noun fem. *native land,* 13.

patricii, -orum, noun masc. plur. *patricians, nobles,* 24.

patrius, -a, -um, adj. *belonging to a father,* 5.

pauci, -ae, -a, adj. plur. *few,* 14.

paulum, noun of quantity, *a little,* 8.

pavor, -oris, noun masc. *fear, panic,* 10.

pax, pācis, noun fem. *peace,* 1.

pectus, -oris, noun neut. *breast, chest,* 19.

pecūnia, -ae, noun fem. *money,* 9.

pecus, -oris, noun neut. *cattle,* 16.

pedes, -itis, noun masc. *foot-soldier,* 13.

pedester, -tris, -tre, adj. *on foot,* 19.

pello, -ere, pepuli, pulsum, vb. tr. *drive away,* 5: *drive back,* 24.

penātes, -ium, noun masc. plur. *household gods,* 22.

pendeo, -ere, pependi, vb. intr. *hang,* 2.

penes, prep. foll. by accus. *in the power of, in the hands of,* 20.

penetro, -are, -avi, -atum, vb. intr. *penetrate, make one's way,* 16.

penitus, advb. *deeply, far within,* 6.

per, prep. foll. by accus. *through, throughout,* of place and time, 1, 6: *by means of,* 10; per gradus, *down the steps* (lit. *by way of* ), 7: cf. per pontem sublicium, 15: iurare per, *swear by,* 10: per causam, *on the excuse of,* 20.

percello, -ere, -culi, -culsum, vb. tr. *dismay, strike with terror,* 7.

percutio, -ere, -cussi, -cussum, vb. tr. 19. See ferio.

pereo, -ire, -ii, vb. intr. *perish,* 13.

perfero, -ferre, -tuli, -lātum, vb. tr. *carry through,* 4: of *carrying a law,* 14.

perficio, -ere, -fēci, -fectum, vb. tr. *accomplish, complete,* 5: *carry out,* 9.

perfugio, -ere, -fūgi, vb. intr. *flee,* 15.

pergo, -ere, perrexi, perrectum, vb. intr. *proceed, go on,* 6, 22.

perīculōsus, -a, -um, adj. *dangerous,* 11.

perīculum, -i, noun neuter, *danger,* 2.

perītus, -a, -um, adj. used with gen. *skilled* (*in*), 6.

permitto, -ere, -mīsi, -missum, vb. tr. *entrust, permit,* 9, 22.

permoveo, -ere, -mōvi, -mōtum, vb. tr. *move greatly,* 4.

peropportūnē, advb. *very opportunely, in the nick of time,* 21.

(in) perpetuum, prepositional phrase, *in perpetuity, for ever,* 18.

persequor, -sequi, -secūtus, vb. tr. *pursue, harry, punish,* 13.

perstringo, -ere, -strinxi, -strictum, vb. tr. *thrill,* 2.

persuādeo, -ere, -suāsi, -suāsum, vb. tr. and intr. *persuade,* 10.

pertempto, -are, -avi, -atum, vb. tr. *work upon,* 12.

perterreo, -ere, -ui, -itum, vb. tr. *frighten exceedingly,* 9.

pervenio, -ire, -vēni, -ventum, vb. intr. *arrive, reach* (with ad), 6.

pēs, pedis, noun masc. *foot;* pedem refero, *retreat,* 19.

pessimus, -a, -um, adj., superlative to malus, *most wicked,* 6.

pestis, -is, noun fem. *destruction,* 24.

peto, -ere, -īvi, -ītum, vb. tr. *seek,* 4; peto ab, *beg, entreat,* 18.

piger, -gra, -grum, pigrior, pigerrimus, adj. *lazy,* 3.

pignus, -oris, noun neut. *pledge, guarantee,* 12.

placeo, -ere, -ui, -itum, vb. intr. *please;* placet ut, *it is resolved that,* 12: with inf. 20.

placidē, advb. *quietly, with pleasure,* 12.

plānus, -a, -um, adj. *level,* 5.

plēbēius, -a, -um, adj. *plebeian,* 21.

plebs, plēbis, noun fem. *populace, lower orders,* 1.

plūs, plūris, noun of quantity, comparative to multum, *more,* 15.

poena, -ae, noun fem. *penalty, punishment,* 10.

**polliceor,** -eri, -itus, vb. tr. *promise,* 10.

**pōno,** -ere, posui, positum, vb. tr. *place, post,* 15.

**pons,** pontis, noun masc. *bridge,* 15.

**populāris,** -e, adj. *acceptable, popular,* 14.

**populātio,** -onis, noun fem. *devastation,* 20.

**populor,** -ari, -atus, vb. tr. *lay waste,* 22.

**populus,** -i, noun masc. *people,* 6. Plur. *peoples,* 3.

**porta,** -ae, noun fem. *gate,* 10.

**portendo,** -ere, -tendi, -tentum, vb. tr. *foretell, predict,* 6.

**portentum,** -i, noun neut. *portent,* 9.

**porto,** -are, -avi, -atum, vb. tr. *carry,* 4.

**portōrium,** -i, noun neut. *import and export duty,* 15.

**posco,** -ere, poposci, vb. tr. *demand,* 22.

**possum,** posse, potui, vb. intr. *be able,* 9.

**post,** prep. foll. by accus. *after,* 7: *behind,* 16. In paucis post annis, 20, used as an adverb, *a few years later* (lit. *afterwards by a few years*).

**posteā,** advb. *afterwards,* 1.

**posterus,** -a, -um, adj. *next,* 8.

**postquam,** sub. conj. *after that, when,* 3.

**potens,** -entis, adj. *powerful,* 12.

**potestas,** -atis, noun fem. *power,* 21.

**potissimum,** superlative advb. *preferably,* 13.

**potius,** comparative advb. *rather,* 7.

**prae,** prep. foll. by abl. *in front of* (in certain phrases), e.g. prae se tenens, 10: *owing to, on account of* (in conjunction with negatives), 11.

**praecipio,** -ere, -cēpi, -ceptum, vb. tr. *enjoin,* 10.

**praecipuē,** advb. *especially,* 8.

**praeda,** -ae, noun fem. *booty, plunder,* 9.

**praedor,** -ari, -atus, vb. tr. and intr. *plunder,* 24.

**praefero,** -ferre, -tuli, -lātum, vb. tr. *carry in front,* 18.

**praemium,** -i, noun neut. *reward,* 19.

**praesidium,** -i, noun neuter, *protection,* 5: *garrison,* 16: *post, fortification,* 15.

**praesto,** -stare, -stiti, vb. tr. *show:* with fidem, *keep one's word,* 17.

**praesum,** -esse, -fui, vb. intr. *be at the head of, in command of,* 13.

**praetereo,** -ire, -ii, -itum, vb. tr. and intr. *go past,* 24: perf. ptc. *past,* 7.

**praetermitto,** -mittere, -mīsi, -missum, vb. tr. *neglect, omit,* 19.

**praetōrium,** -i, noun neut. *general's tent, headquarters,* 23.

**preces,** -um, noun fem. plur. *prayers,* 22.

**precor,** -ari, -atus, vb. tr. and intr. *pray, entreat,* 15.

**premo,** -ere, pressi, pressum, vb. tr. *press hard, harass,* 10.

**pretium,** -i, noun neut. *price,* 15.

prīmō, adv. *at first*, 3.

prīmōres, -um, noun and adj. masc. plur. *leading men, chief*, 8, 21.

prīmum, advb. *firstly*, 1.

prīmus, -a, -um, adj. *first*, 1: in prīmum, *to the front*, 19.

princeps, -ipis, noun masc. and adj. *leading man*, 8: *first*, 18.

prior, prius, comparative adj. *former*, 3: *earlier, sooner*, 4.

pristinus, -a, -um, adj. *former*, 21.

priusquam, sub. conj. *before*, 22.

prīvātus, -a, -um, *private*, 7: *in a private station*, 11; ex privato, *from place of confinement*, 20.

prō, prep. foll. by abl. *in front of*, 2: *instead of*, 10: *on behalf of*, 14: *as*, 5: *as good as* (pro victis), 13.

prōcēdo, -ere, -cessi, -cessum, vb. intr. *advance, go forward*, 2.

procella, -ae, noun fem. *storm*, 15.

proceres, -um, noun masc. plur. *chief men*, 23.

procul, advb. *far*, 17.

prōdeo, -ire, -ii, -itum, vb. intr. *go forward*, 6.

prōditio, -onis, noun fem. *treachery*, 12.

prōditor, -oris, noun masc. *traitor*, 12.

prōdo, -ere, -didi, -ditum, vb. tr. *betray*, 13.

prōdūco, -ere, -duxi, -ductum, vb. tr. *bring forward*, 17.

proelium, -i, noun neuter, *battle*, 16.

profīciscor, -i, profectus, vb. intr. *set out*, 8.

profugus, -a, -um, adj. *exiled*, 3.

prōgredior, -i, -gressus, vb. intr. *come forward, advance*, 1.

prohibeo, -ere, -ui, -itum, vb. tr. *prevent*, 2.

proinde, advb. *therefore*, 18.

prōlābor, -i, -lapsus, vb. intr. *stumble*, 9: *fall forward*, 10.

promptus, -a, -um, adj. *ready*, 21.

prōnuntio, -are, -avi, -atum, vb. tr. *promise*, 19.

prope, prep. foll. by accus. *near*, 16.

prōpello, -ere, -puli, -pulsum, vb. tr. *drive or push forward*, 16.

propinqui, -orum, noun masc. plur. *relatives*, 17.

proprius, -a, -um, adj. *of one's own*, 24.

propter, prep. foll. by accus. *on account of*, 8.

prōripio, -ere, -ripui, -reptum, vb. tr.; proripio me, *dash forward*, 6.

prōtraho, -ere, -traxi, -tractum, vb. tr. *drag forth*, 8.

prōveho, -ere, -vexi, -vectum, vb. tr. *carry forward*, 24.

prōvideo, -ere, -vīdi, -vīsum, vb. tr. and intr. *exercise foresight*, 21.

prōvolo, -are, -avi, -atum, vb. intr. *dash forward*, 19.

proximus, -a, -um, adj. superlative, *nearest, last, next*, 2, 12.

publicum, -i, noun neut. *the*

*public treasury, public funds,* 18.

**publicus, -a, -um,** adj. *public,* 7.

**pudor, -oris,** noun masc. *shame, honour,* 15.

**puer, -i,** noun masc. *boy,* 5.

**pugna, -ae,** noun fem. *fight,* 2.

**pugno, -are, -avi, -atum,** vb. intr. *fight,* 2.

**purgo, -are, -avi, -atum,** vb. tr. *excuse,* 8.

**puto, -are, -avi, -atum,** vb. tr. *consider, think,* 3.

**quadrātus, -a, -um,** adj. *square,* 13.

**quaero, -ere, quaesīvi, quae-sītum,** vb. tr. *seek, ask,* 9.

**quam,** advb. *than,* 2; *as,* correlative to **tam,** 15: **quam celerrime,** *as quickly as possible,* 10: *how* (qualifying adj. or advb.), 16.

**quamquam,** sub. conj. *although,* 6.

**quando,** advb. interrogative, *when?* also introducing dependent question, 16.

**quantum,** advb. *(as much) as,* correlative to **tantum,** 1; also noun of quantity, *how much?* **quanti?** *at what price?* 21.

**-que,** co-ord. conjunction, *and:* added at the end of the word which it connects with what precedes, 2.

**querella, -ae,** noun fem. *complaint, lament,* 10.

**queror, queri, questus,** vb. tr. and intr. *complain,* 5.

**quī, quae, quod,** relative pronoun, *who,* 1.

**quia,** sub. conjunction, *because,* 2.

**quicumque, quaecumque, quodcumque,** indefinite relative pron. *whosoever:* adj. *whatsoever,* 15.

**quīdam, quaedam, quiddam** (pron.), **quoddam** (adj.), indefinite pron. and adj. *a certain person,* 1.

**quidem,** advb. *indeed,* 8; **ne ...quidem,** *not even,* 5.

**quies, quiētis,** noun fem. *quiet, peace,* 18.

**quiesco, -ere, quiēvi, quiētum,** vb. intr. *to enjoy peace,* 7.

**quiētus, -a, -um,** adj. *quiet, in quiet,* 20.

**quīn,** sub. conjunction, *but that;* **haud dubium est quin,** *there is no doubt that,* 22.

**quis, quae** or **qua, quid,** indefinite pronoun, *anyone,* 11 (used after **si** and **ne**).

**quis** (pron.), **quae, quid:** **quī** (adj.), **quae, quod,** interrogative pronoun and adj. *who? what?* 7.

**quisquam, quicquam,** indefinite pronoun, *anyone* (used after negatives), 10.

**quisque, quaeque, quidque,** pron. *each,* 16, 18.

**quisquis, quidquid,** indefinite relative pronoun, *whoever,* 23.

**quō,** interr. advb. *whither?* 24, v.

**quod,** sub. conj. *because, in that,* 13.

**quondam,** advb. *once upon a time,* 6.

**quoniam,** sub. conj. *since,* 16.

quoque, advb. *also*, 2.

rapio, -ere, -ui, -tum, vb. tr. *hurry*, 19: *seize*, 21.

ratio, -onis, noun fem. *manner*, 1.

recipero, -are, -avi, -atum, vb. tr. *recover*, 11.

recipio, -ere, -cēpi, -ceptum, vb. tr. *recover, receive*, 12, 15.

reconcilio, -are, -avi, -atum, vb. tr. *reconcile*, 8.

reddo,-ere, reddidi, redditum, vb. tr. *give back*, 9: *deliver*, 11: *administer*, 6 (iura reddere): *make, render* (with amicos, infestum), 7, 16.

redeo, -ire, -ii, -itum, vb. intr. *turn back upon, return*, 2: *come round to*, 5.

redigo, -ere, -ēgi, -actum, vb. tr.; in publicum redigere, *pay into the treasury*, 23.

redintegro,-are,-avi,-atum, vb. tr. *renew*, 17.

reditus, -us, noun masc. *return*, 12.

redūco, -ere, -duxi, -ductum, vb. tr. *lead back*, 18.

refero, referre, rettuli, relātum, vb. tr. *bring back, carry back*, 21; pedem or gradum referre, *retreat*, 19 and 23: rem ad senatum referre, *bring up a matter before the senate*, 20: *report* (verba refert), 1.

reficio,-ere,-fēci,-fectum,vb. tr. *make up*, 9.

refugio, -ere, -fūgi, vb. intr. *flee*, 24.

rēgia, -ae, noun fem. *palace*, 4: *royal house*, 5.

rēgīna, -ae, noun fem. *queen*, 5.

rēgius, -a, -um, adj. *royal, regal*, 5: *belonging to a tyrant*, 11.

regno, -are, -avi, -atum, vb. intr. *reign*, 1.

regnum, -i, noun neut. *reign*, 1: *kingdom, throne*, 5.

rego, -ere, rexi, rectum, vb. tr. *direct*, 19.

relinquo,-ere, -līqui,-lictum, vb. tr. *leave, leave behind, abandon*, 6, 15.

remitto,-ere, -mīsi, -missum, vb. tr. *send back*, 17.

removeo, -ere, -mōvi, -mōtum, vb. tr. *remove*, 11.

renovo, -are, -avi, -atum, vb. tr. *renew*, 20.

reor, reri, ratus, vb. tr. *think*, 4.

repello, -ere, reppuli, repulsum, vb. tr. *drive back*, 16.

repentīnus, -a, -um, adj. *sudden*, 15.

repeto,-ere,-petivi,-petitum, vb. tr. *seek again, claim*, 12.

repōno, -ere, -posui, -positum, vb. tr. *place, repose*, 21.

reporto, -are, -avi, -atum, vb. tr. *carry off*; victoriam reportare, *win victory*, 2.

reprehendo, -ere, -ndi, -nsum, vb. tr. *blame, criticize*, 10: *upbraid*, 15.

res, rei, noun fem. *thing, circumstance, sight*, etc., 5; in plur. *effects*, 4: *fortunes*, 5.

resisto,-tere, restiti, vb. intr. *resist*, 11: *make a stand*, 24.

respicio, -ere, -spexi, -spectum, vb. tr. and intr. *look back*, 2: *regard*, 22.

respondeo, -ere, -i, -sponsum, vb. tr. *answer*, 7.

responsum, -i, noun neut. *answer*, 9.

respublica, reipublicae, noun fem. *commonwealth*, 8.

restinguo, -ere, -stinxi, -stinctum, vb. tr. *put out*, 5.

restituo, -uere, -ui, -ūtum, vb. tr. *restore*, 16: *re-form*, 19.

retracto, -are, -avi, -atum, vb. tr. *handle again*, 20.

retraho, -ere, -traxi, -tractum, vb. tr. *drag back*, 16.

retrō, advb. *back*, 22.

retundo, -ere, -tudi, -tūsum, vb. tr. *beat back*, 21.

revehor, -vehi, -vectus, passive of reveho used as deponent, *ride back*, 23.

revertor, -verti, -versus, passive of reverto used as deponent, *return*, 23.

rex, rēgis, noun masc. *king*, 1; plur. *royal family*, 5.

rīpa, -ae, noun fem. *bank*, 16.

rītus, -us, noun masc. *custom, rite*, 4.

rixa, -ae, noun fem. *quarrel, brawl*, 6.

rūmor, -oris, noun masc. *rumour, story*, 24.

rumpo, -ere, rūpi, ruptum, vb. tr. *break*, 15; viam rumpere, *force a way*, 24.

rursus, advb. *again*, 20.

sacellum, -i, noun neut. *shrine*, 3.

sacerdōs, -ōtis, noun common, *priest*, 3.

sacra, -orum, noun neut. plur. *sacred rites*, 3.

sacrificium, -i, noun neut. *sacrifice*, 16.

sacrōsanctus, -a, -um, adj. *sacrosanct, privileged*, 20.

saepe, advb. *often*, 24: comp. *again and again*, 18.

saepio, -ire, saepsi, saeptum, vb. tr. *hedge in, protect*, 15.

sal, salis, noun masc. *salt*, 15.

salūbris, -e, adj. *healthful, beneficial*, 6.

salus, -utis, noun fem. *safety, salvation*, 8.

salvus, -a, -um, adj. *safe*, 18.

sanguis, -guinis, noun masc. *blood*, 6.

satelles, -itis, noun common, *attendant*, 16.

satis, advb. *sufficiently*, 18.

saucius, -a, -um, adj. *wounded*, 19.

saxum, -i, noun neut. *stone*, 8.

scelerātus, -a, -um, adj. *criminal*, 10.

scelus, -eris, noun neut. *crime*, 6.

scio, scire, scivi, scitum, vb. tr. *know*, 22.

sciscitor, -ari, -atus, vb. tr. and intr. *enquire, make enquiries*, 9.

scrība, -ae, noun masc. *clerk*, 16.

scūtum, -i, noun neuter, *shield*, 15.

sē, gen. sui, personal pronoun, reflexive, 3rd pers. *himself*, etc. 4.

sēcēdo, -ere, -cessi, -cessum, vb. intr. *withdraw*, 20.

sēcessio, -onis, noun fem. *withdrawal*, 21.

sēcrētum, -i, noun neut. *secret place*, 5.

sēcrētus, -a, -um, adj. *secret*, 7.

sēcum, abl. of se followed by cum, *with him(self)*, etc., 4.

secundum, prep. followed by accus. *after*, 18.

secundus, -a, -um, adj. *favourable, propitious*, 15.

secūris, acc. secūrim, abl. secūrī, noun fem. *axe*, 6.

sed, coord. conj. *but*, 2.

sedeo, -ere, sēdi, sessum, vb. intr. *sit*, 6: *sit still*, 16.

sēdes, sēdis, noun fem. *seat, throne*, 6.

sēditio, -onis, noun fem. *riot, sedition*, 3.

segnius, advb., comparative to segniter, *more slowly, less energetically*, 23.

semper, advb. *always*, 16.

senātus, -us, noun masc. *senate*, 8.

senectus, -utis, noun fem. *old age*, 7.

sententia, -ae, noun fem. *opinion*, 21.

sentio, -ire, sensi, sensum, vb. tr. *feel, be aware of, realize*, 12, 16.

sepelio, -ire, -ivi, sepultum, vb. tr. *bury*, 8.

sequor, sequi, secūtus, vb. tr. *follow, pursue*, 2.

sērius, advb., comparative to sērō, *later*, 12.

sermo, -onis, noun masc. *conversation, discourse*, 7.

serva, -ae, noun fem. *female slave*, 7.

servitus, -utis, noun fem. *slavery*, 15.

servo, -are, -avi, -atum, vb. tr. *observe, keep*, 8: *save*, 15.

servus, -i, noun masc. *male slave*, 7.

sex, indeclinable adj. *six*, 24.

sī, subord. conjunction, *if*, 6.

sīc, advb. *thus*, 3.

sicco, -are, -avi, -atum, vb. tr. *dry, drain*, 5.

sīcut, sub. conj. *just as*, 6.

signum, -i, noun neut. *signal*, 19; plur. *standards*, 20.

similis, -e, similior, simillimus, adj. *like*, 3.

simul, advb. *at the same time*, 2; simul...simul, *both...and*, 10.

simul atque, sub. conj. *as soon as*, 10.

simulo, -are, -avi, -atum, vb. tr. *pretend*, 6.

sine, prep. foll. by abl. *without*, 5.

singuli, -ae, -a, plur. adj. *one each*, 2.

sino, -ere, sīvi, situm, vb. tr. *allow*, 4; perf. ptc. situs, *situated*, 16.

sīve...sīve, subord. conj. *whether...or* (conditional), 18.

socer, soceri, noun masc. *father-in-law*, 8.

societas, -atis, noun fem. *alliance*, 8: *association*, 12.

sodālis, -is, noun common, *companion*, 24.

sōl, sōlis, noun masc. *sun*, 8.

solidus, -a, -um, adj. *whole, entire*, 11.

solium, -i, noun neut. *throne*, 7.

sollicitus, -a, -um, adj. *anxious, full of anxiety*, 1.

sōlum, advb. *only,* 2.

sōlus, -a, -um, gen. solius, adj. *alone, solitary,* 8.

somnus, -i, noun masc. *sleep,* 5.

sōpio, -ire, -ivi, -itum, vb. tr. *stun,* 6.

soror, -oris, noun fem. *sister,* 7.

sors, sortis, noun fem. *chance, lot,* 9: *answer of an oracle,* III.

sospes, sospitis, adj. *safe,* 24.

spatium, -i, noun neut. *distance,* 2.

species, -ei, noun fem. *appearance,* 9.

spectāculum, -i, noun neut. *sight,* 14.

spectātus, -a, -um, adj. *excellent,* 10: *approved,* 14.

specto, -are, -avi, -atum, vb. tr. and intr. *watch, look at,* 2: *look,* 7, 9.

specus, -us, noun masc. *cave,* 9.

sperno, -ere, sprēvi, sprētum, vb. tr. *despise,* 8.

spēro, -are, -avi, -atum, vb. tr. *hope,* 3: *hope for,* 4: *expect,* 12.

spēs, spei, noun fem. *hope,* 2.

spolia, -orum, noun neut. plur. *spoils,* 13.

spolio, -are, -avi, -atum, vb. tr. *despoil, rob,* 2.

(suā) sponte, advb. *of one's own accord,* 23.

statim, advb. *immediately,* 16.

statio, -onis, noun fem. *post, guard,* 15.

statīva, -orum, noun neut. plur. *stationary camp,* 10.

statua, -ae, noun fem. *statue,* 17.

statuo, -ere, -i, -ūtum, vb. tr. *determine,* 5.

stīpendium, -i, noun neut. *pay,* 16.

sto, stare, steti, vb. intr. *stand,* 13.

strēnuus, -a, -um, adj. *energetic,* 4.

struo, -ere, struxi, structum, vb. tr. *construct, be busy with,* 12.

studeo, -ere, -ui, vb. tr. *be eager for,* 9.

stultitia, -ae, noun fem. *folly,* 9.

stupeo, -ere, -ui, vb. intr. *be amazed, be struck dumb,* 24.

suādeo, -ere, suāsi, suāsum, vb. tr. and intr. *urge,* 10.

sub, prep. foll. by abl. (of rest), *under,* 4.

subeo, -ire, -ii, -itum, vb. tr. and intr. *undertake:* come *up,* 24.

subicio, -ere, -iēci, -iectum, vb. tr. *put below, put at the foot of,* 14.

subitō, advb. *suddenly,* 1.

subitus, -a, -um, adj. *sudden,* 6.

sublātus. Cf. tollo, 15.

sublicius, -a, -um, adj. *resting on piles,* 15.

sublīmis, -e, adj. *aloft, up on high,* 1.

submitto, -ere -mīsi, -missum, vb. tr. *lower,* 14.

subrogo, -are, -avi, -atum, vb. tr. *appoint in the place of,* 14.

subsidiārius, -a, -um, adj. *in reserve,* 19.

**subsidium**, -i, noun neut. *relief*, 20; **subsidio venire**, *come to the help of*, 24; plur. *reserves*, 23.

**subtraho**, -ere, -traxi, -tractum, vb. tr. *withdraw*, 23.

**succēdo**, -ere, -cessi, -cessum, vb. intr. *succeed to*, 1.

**succurro**, -ere, -curri, -cursum, vb. intr. *occur to*, 22.

**sufficio**, -ere, -fēci, -fectum, vb. tr. and intr. *suffice*, 9: *appoint in the place of*, 14.

**sum**, esse, fui, vb. intr. *be*, 1.

**summus**, -a, -um, adj. superlative, *greatest, utmost*, 2: *the top of*, 14.

**sūmo**, -ere, sumpsi, sumptum, vb. tr. *take, take up*; **poenas sumere**, *exact a penalty*, 10.

**sumptus**, -us, noun masc. *expense*, 18.

**super**, prep. foll. by accus. *above, on the top of*, 2.

**superbia**, -ae, noun fem. *pride*, 10.

**superbus**, -a, -um, adj. *proud, arrogant, tyrannical*, 8.

**superior**, -oris, adj. comparative, *upper*, 6: *superior*, 24.

**supernē**, advb. *from above*, 2.

**supero**, -are, -avi, -atum, vb. tr. *overcome, get past*, 24.

**superstes**, -stitis, adj. *surviving*, 14.

**supersum**, -esse, -fui, vb. intr. *be left over*, 2: *survive*, 4.

**supervenio**, -ire, -vēni, -ventum, vb. intr. *turn up, come upon the scenes*, 12.

**suppedito**, -are, -avi, -atum, vb. tr. *supply*, 24.

**supplex**, supplicis, adj. *suppliant*, 13.

**supplicium**, -i, noun neut. *punishment*, 13.

**suprā**, prep. foll. by accus. *above*, 14: *beyond*, 17.

**surdus**, -a, -um, adj. *deaf*, 12.

**surgo**, -ere, surrexi, surrectum, vb. intr. *rise, get up*, 22.

**suspectus**, -a, -um, perf. ptc. of suspicio used in the sense of *suspected*, 14.

**suspicio**, -onis, noun fem. *suspicion*, 14.

**sustineo**, -ere, -ui, -tentum, vb. tr. *withstand*, 15: *uphold*, 23.

**suus**, -a, -um, poss. adj. *his, their, his own, their own*, 8.

**tālis**, -e, adj. *such*, 20.

**tam**, advb. *so*, 5.

**tamen**, advb. *nevertheless*, 7.

**tandem**, advb. *at length*, 6.

**tantum**, advb. and noun of quantity, *so much*, 1, 15; advb. *only*, 12.

**tantus**, -a, -um, adj. *so great*, 6.

**tēcum**, abl. of tu followed by cum, *with you*, 22.

**tēlum**, -i, noun neut. *weapon*, 6.

**temerē**, advb. *rashly*, 21.

**temeritas**, -atis, noun fem. *recklessness*, 24.

**tempestas**, -atis, noun fem. *storm*, 1.

**templum**, -i, noun neut. *temple*, 9.

**tempto**, -are, -avi, -atum, vb. tr. *make trial of*, 3.

**tempus**, -oris, noun neut. *time*; in plur. *times*, 3: *dates*, 18; in tempore, *in the nick of time*, 24.

**teneo**, -ere, -ui, vb. tr. *hold*, 7: *keep*, 15.

**tergum**, -i, noun neut. *back*, v; a tergo, *behind*, 15.

**tero**, -ere, trīvi, trītum, vb. tr. *wear away, waste*, 23.

**terra**, -ae, noun fem. *land, earth*, 1.

**terribilis**, -e, adj. *terrible, awful*, 9.

**terror**, -oris, noun masc. *terror, alarm*, 7.

**tertius**, -a, -um, adj. *third*, 2.

**testāmentum**, -i, noun neut. *will*, 4.

**timeo**, -ere, -ui, vb. tr. *fear*, 12.

**timor**, -oris, noun masc. *fear*, 20.

**tollo**, -ere, sustuli, sublātum, vb. tr. *take up*, 4: *raise*, 15.

**tonitrus**, -us, noun masc. *thunder*, 1.

**torreo**, -ere, -ui, tostum, vb. tr. *burn, scorch*, 16.

**tot**, indeclinable adj. *so many*, 18.

**totiens**, advb. *so many times*, 21.

**tōtus**, -a, -um, gen. totius, adj. *whole*, 11; toti, plur. *wholly*, 10.

**trabea**, -ae, noun fem. *robe of state*, 6.

**trādo**, -ere, -didi, -ditum, vb. tr. *hand over*, 10.

**trādūco**, -ere, -duxi, -ductum, vb. tr. *lead across, transfer*, 8.

**traho**, -ere, traxi, tractum, vb. tr. *drag along*, 2.

**trāicio**, -ere, -iēci, -iectum, vb. tr. *pierce, run through*, 19.

**trāno**, -are, -avi, -atum, vb. intr. *swim across*, 15.

**trans**, prep. followed by ac cus. *across*, 16.

**transeo**, -ire, -ii, -itum, vb. tr. *cross*, 15.

**transfero**, -ferre, -tuli, -lātum, vb. tr. *transfer, remove*, 11.

**transfīgo**, -ere, -fixi, -fixum, vb. tr. *pierce, run through*, 13.

**transfuga**, -ae, noun masc. *deserter*, 16.

**transilio**, -ilire, -ilui, vb. tr. *jump across*, 23.

**trecenti**, -ae, -a, plur. adj. *three hundred*, 16.

**trepidus**, -a, -um, adj. *excited, agitated*, 7.

**trēs**, trium, plur. adj. *three*, 2.

**triārii**, -orum, noun masc. plur. *reserve troops*, 23.

**tribūnal**, -alis, noun neut. *platform, tribunal*, 16.

**tribūnīcius**, -a, -um, adj. *belonging to a tribune*, 21.

**tribūnus**, -i, noun masc. *plebeian magistrate, tribune*, 20.

**tribūtum**, -i, noun neut. *tax*, 15.

**trigemini**, -orum, noun masc. plur. *three brothers born at a birth*, 2.

**triumpho**, -are, -avi, -atum, vb. intr. *triumph*, 13.

**tū**, tui, personal pronoun of 2nd pers. *thou, you*, 6.

tueor, tueri, tuitus, vb. **tr.** *protect*, 20.

tuli. See fero.

tum, advb. *then*, 2.

tumultuōsus, -a, -um, adj. *alarming*, 20.

tumultus, -us, noun masc. *tumult, fuss*, 10.

turba, -ae, noun fem. *crowd*, 15.

turma, -ae, noun fem. *squadron*, 23.

tūtēla, -ae, noun fem. *maintenance*, 1.

tūtor, -oris, noun masc. *guardian*, 4.

tūtor, -ari, -atus, vb. tr. *protect*, 8.

tūtus, -a, -um, adj. *safe*, 9; tūtum, *safe place*, 15.

tuus, -a, -um, poss. adj. *your*, 6.

tyrannus, -i, noun masc. *despot*, 21.

ubi, subord. conjunction, *when*, 3: *where*, 2.

ubique, advb. *everywhere*, 10.

ullus, -a, -um, gen. ullius, adj. *any* (used after negatives), 14.

ultor, -oris, noun masc. *avenger*, 13.

ultrā, advb. *further*, 19.

undique, advb. *on all sides, from all sides*, 15.

ūnus, -a, -um, gen. unius, adj. *one*, 2.

urbs, -is, noun fem. *city*, 1.

ut, subord. conjunction, *as*, 5, 24: *in order that*, 7: introducing clause of dependent desire, 10, clause of result, 14; *when*, v.

uter, -tra, -trum, gen. utrius,

interrog. adj. and pronoun, *which of two?* 9.

uterque, utraque, utrumque, gen. utriusque, adj. and pron. *each of two*, 13; in plur. *each of two parties*, 17.

utique, advb. *at any rate*, 21.

ūtor, ūti, ūsus, vb. intr. used with abl. *use, make use of*, 9.

utrimque, advb. *on both sides*, 2.

utrum...an, interrogative adverbs, *whether...or*, 22.

uxor, -oris, noun fem. *wife*, 3.

vādo, -ere, vāsi, vāsum, vb. intr. *go, make one's way*, 15.

vagor, -ari, -atus, vb. intr. *wander, stray about*, 16.

valeo, -ere, -ui, vb. intr. *be worth, hold good*, 12.

vallum, -i, noun neuter, *rampart*, 20.

vastus, -a, -um, adj. *empty*, 24.

vehemens, -entis, adj. *fierce, vehement*, 7.

vehementer, advb. *fiercely*, in superl. 22.

vehiculum, -i, noun neuter, *carriage, conveyance*, 12.

vel, coord. conj. *or*, 10; vel... vel, *either...or*, 5.

vēlo, -are, -avi, -atum, vb. tr. *wrap*, 21.

velut, advb. *just as*, 24, v.

vendo, -ere, -didi, -ditum, vb. tr. *sell*, 15.

vēneo, -ire, -ii, -itum, vb. intr. *be sold*, 15.

venio, -ire, vēni, ventum, vb. intr. *come*, 4; ad extremum venire, *come to the worst possible pass*, 23.

**verbum,** -i, noun neut. *word,* 1.

**vērē,** advb. *truly,* 5.

**verēcundia,** -ae, noun fem. *feeling of shame,* 18.

**vereor,** vereri, veritus, vb. tr. *fear,* 16.

**vērō,** coord. conjunction, *but, however,* 2: sometimes as emphasizing advb. *indeed;* **tum vero,** *then indeed,* 7.

**versor,** versari, versatus, pass. of **verso** used as deponent, *turn about, move about,* 23: *be, be circumstanced,* 16.

**vertex,** -icis, noun masc. *top,* 24.

**verto,** -ere, -i, versum, vb. tr. *turn,* 10.

**vērus,** -a, -um, adj. *true,* 24; **re verā,** *in reality,* 3.

**vester,** -tra, -trum, poss. adj. *your,* 14.

**vestibulum,** -i, noun neut. *porch,* 6.

**vestis,** -is, noun fem. *garment, clothes,* 10.

**veto,** -are, vetui, vetitum, vb. tr. *forbid,* 5.

**vetus,** gen. veteris, adj. *old,* 21.

**via,** -ae, noun fem. *path, way,* 13.

**victor,** -oris, noun masc. and adj. *victor, victorious,* 2.

**victōria,** -ae, noun fem. *victory,* 2.

**video,** -ere, vīdi, vīsum, vb. tr. *see,* 2. In passive, *seem,* 8.

**vīlis,** -e, adj. *worthless,* 16.

**vinclum,** -i, noun neut. *chain,* 12.

**vinco,** -ere, vīci, victum, vb.

**tr.** and intr. *conquer, overpower,* 3, 24.

**violentus,** -a, -um, adj. *violent, headstrong,* 7.

**violo,** -are, -avi, -atum, vb. tr. *outrage,* 14.

**vir,** viri, noun masc. *man,* 1: *husband,* 4.

**vīres,** -ium, noun fem. plur. *strength,* 2.

**virga,** -ae, noun fem. *rod,* 13.

**virgo,** -inis, noun fem. *maiden,* 17.

**virītim,** advb. *man by man,* 7.

**virtus,** -utis, noun fem. *valour,* 2: *worth,* 15.

**vīs,** acc. **vim,** noun fem. *force, violence,* 3: *quantity,* 21.

**vīvo,** -ere, vixi, victum, vb. intr. *live,* 6.

**vīvus,** -a, -um, adj. *living,* 7.

**vix,** advb. *scarcely,* 8.

**voco,** -are, -avi, -atum, vb. tr. *call,* 6.

**volgus,** volgi, noun neuter, *common people, crowd,* 14.

**volnero,** -are, -avi, -atum, vb. tr. *wound,* 2.

**volnus,** -eris, noun neut. *wound,* 2.

**volo,** velle, volui, vb. tr. *wish,* 5.

**voltus,** -us, noun masc. *face, countenance,* 13.

**voluntas,** -atis, noun fem. *wish, good-will,* 7.

**vōs,** personal pron. plur. of **tu,** *you,* 8.

**voveo,** -ere, vōvi, vōtum, vb. tr. *vow,* 19.

**vox,** vōcis, noun fem. *voice,* 7: *utterance,* 9.

# ENGLISH-LATIN REFERENCES

NOTE. *The* REFERENCES *are to the* FIRST OCCURRENCE *of the word required or to its* FIRST OCCURRENCE *in a* PARTICULAR MEANING. SEVERAL REFERENCES *to* ONE WORD *imply that there are* SEVERAL LATIN EQUIVALENTS *for it.*

*If a* WORD *is required in an* EXERCISE *earlier than it occurs in the* TEXT, *the* LATIN *for it is supplied and the actual occurrence* NOTED: *a very few* COMMON WORDS *which do not occur at all are also given.*

*able* (be). See *can*.
*about* =in the neighbourhood of, 5; =concerning, 1.
*acceptable*, 14.
*accustomed* (be), 12.
*address*, 6.
*admit*, admitto, -ere, -misi, -missum.
*advance*, 1, 2; *advance furiously against one another*, 13.
*afraid (be)*, 12, 16.
*after* (prep.) 7, (conj.) 3.
*afterwards*, 1.
*again*, iterum, 21; rursus, 20.
*against*, **2**, **7**; *against one another* = among themselves, 9.
*aid* (vb.), 13; (noun), *lend* or *render aid*, 13.
*alarm*, terreo, -ere, -ui, -itum.
*all*, 1; *all over the place*, passim, 21.
*allow*, 4: permitto, -ere, -misi, -missum, 22.
*alone*, 8.
*already*, 2.
*also*, 2.
*although*, 6.
*always*, semper, 16.

*ambassador*, 12.
*ambush*, 5.
*and*, 1, 2, 4; *and not* (in clauses of purpose, etc.), 9.
*announce*, 1.
*another*, 2.
*answer* (vb.), 7, (noun), 9.
*anxiety*. See *anxious*.
*anxious*, 1; *be anxious to*: see *wish*.
*appeal to*, 6.
*appear*, 5, 8.
*appoint*, 11; *on the appointed day*, 21.
*apprehension*, 8.
*approach* =be at hand, 15.
*appropriate*, 3.
*arms*, 2.
*army*, 2.
*arouse*, 5.
*arrest*, 6.
*arrive*, 8.
*ask*. See *entreat*; *ask a question*, 9, 17.
*asleep* (be), 5.
*assembly*, 8, 11.
*assert*. See *say*.
*assume* (a burden), 24.
*as to* =concerning, 1; =that,

introducing clause of re-
sult, 14.

*at* =near, 19; *at dawn,* 1; *at
first,* 3; *at last,* 6; *at once* =
all together, 2; *at once* =
immediately, 7.

*attack* (noun), 15.

*attack* (vb.) (places), oppugno,
20; (people), 2.

*attendant,* 6.

*avenged* (be avenged on), 13.

*axe,* 6.

*bad,* malus, -a, -um, 15.

*baffled* (be), 13.

*band,* 19.

*banish,* 10, 11.

*banishment* (procure banishment of). See *drive out.*

*bar* (a road), 10; *bar the way
with,* 15.

*battle,* 16.

*be,* 1; *be of good cheer,* 6.

*bear away,* 11.

*beautiful,* pulcher, -ra, -rum.

*because,* 2.

*become,* fio, fieri, factus sum,
20.

*before* (conj.) 22; (prep.) 8.

*beg.* See *entreat.*

*begin,* 3; *begin to fight,* 2.

*behead,* 13.

*belong* (to). See *be.*

*betray,* 13.

*betroth,* 5.

*better.* See *good.*

*between,* 2.

*bid,* 4; *bid not* : see *forbid.*

*bind,* 13.

*blow,* 6.

*body,* 2; *in a body,* 23.

*book,* 1.

*booty,* 9.

*both,* 6; *both...and,* 3.

*boy,* 5.

*brave,* 4.

*bravely,* fortiter.

*break,* 15; *break down,* 15.

*bridge,* 15.

*bring about a reconciliation
between,* 8; *bring about the
ruin of,* 8.

*bring back,* reduco, -ere, -duxi,
-ductum, 18.

*bring down,* 14; *bring down a
weapon upon,* 6.

*bring forward,* 17.

*bring news.* See *announce.*

*bring up,* 21.

*brother,* 2.

*build,* 9.

*burden,* 15.

*bury,* 8.

*but,* 2.

*by* (of agent), 1; *by sunset,* 8.

*bystanders* =those who had
taken their stand round,
8.

*call,* 2, 6.

*camp,* 2.

*can* =be able, possum, posse,
potui, 9.

*capture,* 3.

*carry down,* 10; *carry out*
(instructions), 9; *carry forward* (with them), 23.

*catch sight of,* conspicio, -ere,
-spexi, -spectum, 24; conspicor, -ari, -atus, 19.

*cattle,* 16.

*cavalry,* 13.

*centre,* 1.

*chains,* 8.

*chance.* See *opportunity.*

*chieftain, chief man,* 8.

*children,* 4, 5.

*choose,* lego, -ere, legi, lectum,

21 ; *not to choose*: see *un-willing*.
*citizen*, 1.
*city*, 1.
*clan*, 10.
*clear* (be), 5, 18.
*clearly-marked-out*, 13.
*cloud*, 1.
*collapse*, 2.
*colleague*, 11.
*collect* (conveyances),    4; (spoils), 13.
*combat* (engage in), 2 ; (noun), 2.
*come*, 4; *come against:* see *attack; come forward*, 1, 2 ; *come in due succession*, 5.
*command* (under the command of), 13.
*commander-in-chief*, 19.
*common people*, 1, 14.
*companion*, 7.
*comrade*, 7.
*conceive contempt for*, 24.
*conduct* (funeral of), 13.
*conquer*, 3.
*consider* (to be), 3.
*conspiracy:* see *thing:* or 20.
*conspirator*, 12.
*consul*, 10.
*consulship*, 11.
*consult*, 6.
*consultation*, 7.
*conversation*, 7.
*conveyance*, 12.
*corn*, 15.
*council*, 8.
*country* (native), 13.
*courage*, 2.
*courageous*. See *brave*.
*coward(ly)*, 7.
*crash*, 1.
*crime*, 6.

*cross*, 15.
*crush*, 12.
*cultivate*, colo, -ere, -ui, cultum (21 in different sense).

*dagger*, 10.
*dangerous*, 11.
*dare*, 7.
*dash forward*, 19.
*dates*, 18.
*daughter*, 8.
*dawn* (at), 1.
*day*, 6.
*dead*, 3.
*dear*. See *dearness*.
*dearness*, 16.
*death*, 1.
*decide*, 6.
*decisive* (victory), insignis, 13.
*declare:* see *state*; (as king), 7.
*defeat*. See *conquer*.
*defence* (in defence of). See *defend*.
*defend*, defendo, -ere, -di, -sum, 20.
*deliver duly*, 11.
*demand*, posco, -cre, poposci, 22.
*depart*, 1, 11.
*deprive of*, 19.
*despatch* = kill, 2.
*despise*, 8, 24.
*determine*, 4.
*dictator*, 18.
*die*, 2, 3; *in a dying condition*, 10.
*disband*, 20.
*disclose*, 16.
*disgrace*, 5, 21.
*dismount*, 19.
*displease*, 12.
*do*, 6.
*drag back*, 16.
*drain*, 5.

*draw aside*, 5.
*dreadful*, 7.
*dress* (noun), 10.
*dressed very much alike*, 16.
*drive away*, 5; *drive out*, 11.
*drown*, 8.
*duties*, 6.

*earth*, 1.
*easily*, 1.
*effort* (make great), 3.
*either—or*, 20.
*elevated*, 4, 24.
*elsewhere* = elsewhither, 9.
*emissary*. See *ambassador*.
*endure*, 21.
*enemy* (public), 2.
*engage in combat*, 2.
*engagement*. See *fight*.
*enlist*, 20.
*enquire*, 9.
*enrol*, 3.
*enter*, intro, -are, -avi, -atum, 16.
*entreat*, 10, 15; *entreat urgently*, 11.
*entrust*, 6.
*escape*, effugio, -ere, -fugi.
*even*, vel; *not even*, 5.
*excellent*, 4.
*excuse* (vb.), 8.
*execute*. See *kill* or *behead*.
*exhort*, 10, 19.
*exile* (noun), 10; *be in, go into*, 10.
*exist*. See *be*.
*existence* (be in), exsto, -are.
*expect*. See *hope*.
*express pity for*, 13.

*ace* (in the face of), = against, 2.
*fall*, 9; *fall under* (suspicion), 14; *fall dead*, 2.

*false*, 4.
*fame*, 4.
*family*: see *clan*, also 24; *royal family*, 5.
*famous*, 2.
*father*, 3; *belonging to a father*, 5; *father-in-law*, 8.
*favour*, 14.
*feeble*, 14.
*feelings*, 12.
*fellow-citizen*. See *citizen*.
*fickle*, 14.
*fields*, 7.
*fiercely contested*, 19.
*fight* (noun), 2, 16; (vb.), 2.
*finally*, 3.
*find*, 10.
*fire* (noun), 6; (vb.) *fire the courage of*, 23.
*first*, 1; *at first*, 3.
*flame*, 5.
*flee*, 2, 6.
*fling down*, 7.
*food*, cibus, -i.
*fool(ish)*, stultus, -a, -um.
*for* (conj.) 1; (prep.) = with a view to, 9.
*forbid*, 5.
*force* (noun), 3; = army, 2.
*form*. See *be*.
*fortress*, 14.
*forum*, 5.
*found*, 1.
*free* (adj.), 18; (vb.) *free from*, 11, 13.
*freedom*, libertas, -atis, 11.
*fresh*, 3.
*friend*, amicus, -i, 7, 10.
*friendship*, 4.
*from*, 5.
*front* (to the), 19.
*fugitive*. See *flee*.
*funeral*, 18.

*gain*(praise), 21; (victory), **2.**
*gate*, 10.
*generous*, 4.
*get to.* See *reach.*
*girl* =maiden, 17.
*give*, 7; *give a public funeral
to*, 18; *give as companion to*,
9; *give attention to*, 24; *give
in marriage*, 7; *give no rest
to*, 7; *give a shout*: see
*raise*; *give out*, 4.
*go*, eo, ire, ii, itum, 13; *go away,
go up*, 1; *go for nothing*, 7;
*go into exile*, 10.
*god*, 6.
*good*, bonus, -a, -um; =*en-
couraging*, 4.
*grandson*, 3.
*great*, 1.
*guarantee*, 12.
*guard*, 8; *be on guard*, 15.
*guardian*, 4.

*hand* (*right*), 16.
*happen*, 10; *as it happened, it
happened that*, 2.
*harangue*, 6.
*hardly*, 8.
*hardships.* See *bad.*
*hasten*, 10.
*have*, 7.
*he*, 1.
*head*, 1.
*hear*, 8.
*heart*, 10. See also *feelings.*
*help* (noun), auxilium, -i, 11;
(vb.) auxilium ferre: see
also adiuvo, -are, -iuvi,
-iutum, 13.
*hereupon*, 2.
*high*, 4; *a high rate*: see *great*;
*on high*, 1.
*hill*, 14.
*himself, herself, itself*, etc.,

emphasizing adj., **4;** reflexive pronoun, 4.
*hinder*, 11.
*his, her, their* (*own*), 8.
*hold* (conversation, etc.), 7.
*home, at home*, 14; *from home*,
12; (*to*) *home*, 8, in sing.
domum.
*honour* (noun), 5, 14.
*hope* (noun), 2; (vb.) =*have
hopes*, 3; *hope for*, 4.
*horse*, 13; *horse-soldier*, 13.
*hostage*, 16.
*hostile*, 13; *in a hostile spirit*,
inimicus, 21.
*house*, 4, 6.
*how* (qualifying adj. or advb.),
16.
*however*, 2, 7.
*how many*, quot (indecl. adj.).
*husband*, 4, 7.

*I*, 1.
*if*, 6.
*immediately*, 7, 8, **16.**
*impregnable*, 14.
*imprison*, 12.
*in* (of place where), 1.
*in office.* See *magistrate.*
*in order that*, 7; *in order that
not*, 7.
*in the neighbourhood of*, 5.
*in turn*, 6.
*inaccuracies*, 18.
*induce.* See *persuade.*
*influence*, vb. 10; noun, 8.
*innocence* (despite his), 8.
*instead of*, 10.
*instructions*, 9.
*international*, 12.
*intervene*, 20.
*into*, 1.
*invade*, 20.
*invincible*, 24.

*nephew* = sister's son, 9.
*nevertheless*, 7.
*new*, 3.
*news* (receive news of). See
   *announce*.
*no one*, 13; (let) *no one*, 20.
*not*, 2; *not even*, 5; *not only*, 2;
   *not yet*, 2.
*now*, *now-a-days*, 13.

*obey*, 18.
*obstacle* (be obstacle to), 11.
*obstinate*, 22.
*obstinately contested*, 19.
*obtain*, 4, 9.
*of*. See *as to*, *out of*.
*omen*, 4.
*on*, 5; *on to*, 6.
*on this occasion*. See *then*.
*one*, 2.
*one day* (in the future), 1.
*one of two*, 2.
*only*, 2.
*onset*, 19.
*open* (vb.), 6, 16.
*openly*, 12.
*opponent*, 2.
*opportunity*, 12.
*oppose*, 11.
*oracle*, 9.
*order*, impero, -are, -avi,
   -atum, 15.
*other*, *the*, 2.
*other* (*some...other*), 6.
*others*, *the* (the rest), 6.
*our*, 5.
*out of* = of, 2.
*overhear*, 12.

*palace*, 4.
*parent*, 1.
*part*, 6; *take part in*, 19.
*parts* = places, 5.
*past*, 7.

*path*, 13.
*patricians*, 20.
*pay* = contribute, 15.
*peace*, 1.
*people*, 6; *peoples*, 3.
*perform*, 6.
*perhaps*, fortasse.
*perish*, 13, 20.
*person* (in his own person).
   See *alone*.
*persuade*, 10.
*pity* (express pity for), 13.
*place*, 2.
*plan*, 7.
*plebeian*, 21; *plebeians*, 1.
*plebs*, 1.
*pledge*, 12.
*plot*, 5.
*plunder* (vb.), 12.
*plunge*, 2.
*populace*, 1.
*portent*, 9.
*position*, *of king*, 5; *of affairs*,
   23.
*post* (vb.), 16, 23.
*postpone*, 8.
*praise*, 21.
*prayers*, 22.
*premature*, 22.
*prepare*, 8.
*present* (*be*), *present oneself*, 8.
*pretend*, 6.
*prevent*, 2.
*previously*, 1.
*price* (at what price), 21.
*priest*, 3.
*procure*, 4.
*promise*, 10.
*property*, 4.
*protect*, 8, 20.
*protection*, 5.
*public*, 7; *public treasury*, 18.
*punish*, 10.
*punishment*, 10.

*purchase* =buy up, 21.
*pursue*, 2.
*put in chains*, 8; *put to death*:
  see *kill*; *put out, extinguish*,
  5; *put out of the way*, 2.

*quantity*, 21.
*queen*, 5.
*quickly*, 6.
*quit*. See *depart*.

*rage* (noun), 8; *in great rage*, 13.
*raise* (*shout*), 15.
*reach*, 4.
*readily*. See *easily*.
*ready*, 18.
*realize*, 3.
*receive* (an attack), 15.
*recognize*, 13.
*recommend*, 10.
*records*, monumenta, -orum.
*recover*, 11, 12.
*refuse*. See *say that...not*.
*regal*, 5.
*reign* (noun and vb.), 1.
*relate*, 1.
*remain*, 11. See also *be*; *be
  left*, 15.
*remain in exile* =be exiles.
*remarkable*, 1.
*remember*, 11.
*remove hastily* =seize, 21.
*render aid*, 13.
*renew*, 20.
*report*, 1.
*resign*, 11.
*resolve*, 12.
*restore* =give back, 9; *restore
  a line*, 16.
*retire*, 1; *retire from* (the
  fight), 19.
*retreat*, 19.
*return*, 2.
*river*, 15.

*road*, 13.
*roam about*, 16.
*rouse*, 7, 23.
*rout*, 13.
*royal*, 5; *royal family*, 5.
*rule*, 15; (over), rego, -ere,
  rexi, rectum, 19.
*run away*. See *flee*.
*run down*, 15.

*safe*, tutus, 9; 15, 24.
*safety* (in), 15.
*said he*, 1; *said they*, inquiunt, 9.
*save*, 15.
*say*, 1; *say that...not*, 5.
*scarce*. See *scarcity*.
*scarcity*, 16.
*scope*, 4.
*scourge*, 13.
*secede*, 20.
*secession*, 21.
*secret*, 7.
*secretary*, 16.
*secure* (adj.), 9.
*secure* (vb.), 4.
*see*, 2; =realize, 3.
*seek*, 4.
*seem*, 8.
*seize* (the throne), 5; *hold of*,
  7; *seize* (cattle), 21.
*sell*, 15.
*senate*, 8.
*senate-house*, 7.
*senators*, 7.
*send*, 7; *send back*, 17; *send
  and tell*, 23.
*serious*, 1.
*seriously*, graviter.
*set out*, 3; *set up below*, 14.
*settle*, 3.
*shepherd*, 6.
*shield*, 13, 15.
*shout*, 5.
*show* (oneself), 23.

*time* (at the), 2.
*times*, 3.
*to*, 2.
*tour* (make tour of), 13.
*towards*, 4.
*town*, oppidum, -i, 21.
*traitor*, 12.
*treachery*, 5.
*trick*, 5, 6.
*troops*. See *soldier*.
*truth*. See *thing*.
*try*, 6.
*turn, in turn,* 6; *turn* (towards), 6.
*two*, 1.
*tyrant*. See *king*.

*unanimous wish*, 4.
*under*, 4.
*understand*, 3.
*undoubtedly*, 5.
*unfortunate*, 22.
*unharmed*, 16.
*unhurt*, 2.
*unless*, 20.
*unlike*, 1.
*unwilling* (be), 7.
*urge*, 10.
*use*, 9.
*utmost*, 2.

*very*. The *very name* = the name itself.
*victory*, 2.
*voice*, 7.

*wage* (war), 2.
*want*: see *wish*; *not to want*: see *unwilling*.
*war*, 1; *make war upon*, 20.
*watch*, 2.
*we*, nōs, 9.
*wealthy*, 15.
*well*, 15.

*when* (relative), 3, 13; (interrogative), 16.
*where* (relative and interrogative), 2.
*whether* (interrogative), 17, *whether...or*, utrum...an, 22.
*which* (relative), 1; (interrogative): see *who*; *which of two*, 9.
*while*, 1.
*who* (relative), 1; (interrogative), 7.
*whole*, 11.
*why*, cur, 21.
*wife*, 3.
*wily*, 6.
*win* = secure, 4; *win over* (to oneself), 4; *win* (victory), 2.
*wish* (be willing, be anxious to), volo, velle, volui, 5.
*wish* (general, unanimous), 4.
*with*, 1.
*without*, 5.
*woman*, 6, 7; *belonging to a woman*, 22.
*wonder*, miror, -ari, -atus.
*wonderful*, 1, 8.
*word*, 1.
*world*, 1.
*worthless*, 16.
*worthy*, 9.
*wound* (noun and vb.), 2.
*wrap*, 1.
*wretched*, 22.
*write*, scribo, -ere, scripsi, scriptum.

*year*, annus, -i, 5.
*yield*, 15.
*you*, 6, 8.
*younger* (the), 7.
*young man*, 5, 12.
*your*, sing., 6; plur. vester, -tra, -trum, 14.

# ADDITIONAL WORDS REQUIRED
## FOR THE *OVID* EXTRACTS

**abrumpo**, -ere, -rūpi, -ruptum, vb. tr. *tear away, rend.*

**aethēr**, -is, noun masc. *upper air.*

**altāria**, -ium, noun neut. plur. *altar.*

**alternus**, -a, -um, adj. *alternate.*

**annuus**, -a, -um, adj. *yearly.*

**aper**, apri, noun masc. *boar.*

**apertus**, -a, -um, adj. *open.*

**armenta**, -orum, noun neut. plur. *herds.*

**arva**, -orum, noun neut. plur. *fields.*

**astra**, -orum, noun neut. plur. *stars.*

**attonitus**, -a, -um, adj. *thunder-struck, startled.*

**aura**, -ae, noun fem. *breeze.*

**canis**, -is, noun comm. *dog.*

**caveo**, -ere, cāvi, cautum, vb. tr. and intr. *beware, beware of.*

**celer**, celeris, celere, adj. *swift.*

**coma**, -ae, noun fem. *hair.*

**coniugium**, -i, noun neut. *marriage.*

**crēdulus**, -a, -um, adj. *credulous, superstitious.*

**cruor**, -oris, noun masc. *blood.*

**dēbeo**, -ere, -ui, -itum, vb. tr. *owe, am obliged, ought.*

**dēcido**, -ere, -i, vb. intr. *fall down.*

**decōrus**, -a, -um, adj. *adorned.*

**destringo**, -ere, -strinxi, -strictum, vb. tr. *draw (a sword).*

**diffugio**, -ere, -fūgi, vb. intr. *flee in different directions.*

**dīrus**, -a, -um, adj. *dread, dreadful.*

**discursus**, -us, noun masc. *running to and fro.*

**dōs**, dōtis, noun fem. *dowry.*

**dōtālis**, -e, adj. *belonging to a dowry.*

**ecce**, interjection, *behold.*

**effundo**, -ere, -fūdi, -fūsum, vb. tr. *pour out.*

**ensis**, -is, noun masc. *sword.*

**evānesco**, -ere, evānui, vb. intr. *vanish.*

**everto**, -ere, -i, -sum, vb. tr. *overthrow.*

**exstimulo**, -are, -avi, -atum, vb. tr. *goad.*

**exstinguo**, -ere, -stinxi, -stinctum, vb. tr. *put out* (fire).

**exta**, -orum, noun neut. plur. *entrails.*

**fax**, facis, noun fem. *torch.*

**fera**, -ae, noun fem. *wild beast.*

**fluo**, -ere, fluxi, vb. intr. *flow.*

**forsitan**, advb. *perhaps.*

**fulmineus**, -a, -um, adj. *like lightning, destructive.*

generōsus, -a, -um, adj.
*well-born.*

gentīlis, -e, adj. *belonging to the same clan.*

grex, gregis, noun masc. *flock, herd.*

hībernus,-a,-um,adj.*wintry.*

horreo, -ere, -ui, vb. intr. *bristle up.*

imber, imbris, noun masc. *shower.*

imitātor, -oris, noun masc. *one who feigns.*

infīrmus, -a, -um, adj. *weak, infirm.*

inhonestus, -a, -um, adj. *dishonourable.*

iniustus, -a, -um, adj. *unjust, dishonourable.*

instinctus, -a, -um, adj. *roused* (ptc. to instinguo, which is not in use).

insum, -esse, -fui, vb. intr. *to be in.*

inultus, -a, -um, adj. *unavenged.*

iuvat, 3rd sing. of iuvare, used impersonally: *it avails.*

lateo, -ere, -ui, vb. intr. *lie hid, lurk.*

lātus, -a, -um, adj. *wide, broad.*

leo, leonis, noun masc. *lion.*

lūna, -ae, noun fem. *moon.*

male, peius, pessime, advb. *badly, unfortunately.*

margo, -inis, noun comm. *border, fringe.*

mercēs, -ēdis, noun fem. *reward, payment.*

montānus, -a, -um, adj. *belonging to the mountains.*

mōtus, -us, noun masc. *motion, movement.*

neco, -are, -avi, -atum, vb. tr. *kill, murder.*

nefandus, -a, -um, adj. *unspeakable, dreadful.*

nefās, noun indeclinable, *impious deed.*

nix, nivis, noun fem. *snow.*

nōbilitas, -atis, noun fem. *nobility, men of noble birth.*

nūbilum, -i, noun neut. *cloud.*

nūmen, -inis, noun neut. *deity, divine will.*

occulo, -ere, -ui, -tum, vb. tr. *conceal.*

ōmen, -inis, noun neut. *omen.*

palūs, -ūdis, noun fem. *marsh.*

passus, -us, noun masc. *step.*

perago, -ere, -ēgi, -actum, vb. tr. *complete, accomplish.*

perdo, -ere, -didi, -ditum, vb. tr. *destroy.*

perfīdus, -a, -um, adj. *treacherous.*

pius, -a, -um, adj. *good, dutiful.*

plāco, -are, -avi, -atum, vb. tr. *appease.*

pluviālis, -e, adj. *heavy with, swollen by, rain.*

prōcumbo, -ere,-cubui,-cubitum, vb. intr. *fall forward.*

profīteor, -eri, -fessus, vb. tr.: the perf. ptc. is used in v in a passive sense, *volunteered*.

**prōles**, -is, noun fem. *offspring*.

**prōnus**, -a, -um, adj. *prone, flat on one's face*.

**propero**, -are, -avi, -atum, vb. tr. and intr. *hurry*.

**prōsilio**, -ire, -ui, vb. tr. *dash forward*.

**pulcher**, -ra, -rum, adj. *beautiful*.

**quīlibet**, **quaelibet**, **quidlibet**, pron. *anyone at all*.

**rapax**, -ācis, adj. *swift, rushing*.

**rārus**, -a, -um, adj. *far apart, here and there*.

**resto**, -are, -stiti, vb. intr. *remain, be left*.

**rubeo**, -ere, vb. intr. *be red*.

**ruo**, -ere, -i, vb. intr. *rush*.

**rūpes**, -is, noun fem. *rock*.

**saepes**, -is, noun fem. *hedge*.

**sapiens**, -entis, adj. *wise*.

**sata**, -orum, noun neut. plur. *crops*.

**sceptrum**, -i, noun neut. *sceptre*.

**sīdo**, -ere, sēdi, sessum, vb. intr. *settle down, take a seat*.

**silva**, -ae, noun fem. *wood*.

**simplex**, -icis, adj. *guileless*.

**sinister**, -tra, -trum, adj. *on the left hand*.

**soleo**, -ere, solitus, vb. intr. *be accustomed*.

**spargo**, -ere, sparsi, sparsum, vb. tr. *scatter*.

**sterno**, -ere, strāvi, strātum, vb. tr. *lay low*.

**stultus**, -a, -um, adj. *foolish*.

**suprēmus**, -a, -um, adj. superlative, *last*.

**suscipio**, -ere, -cēpi, -ceptum, vb. tr. *undertake, take on oneself*.

**tango**, -ere, tetigi, tactum, vb. tr. *touch, reach*.

**tego**, -ere, texi, tectum, vb. tr. *cover, conceal*.

**tenuis**, -e, adj. *thin*.

**tepeo**, -ere, vb. intr. *be warm*.

**tingo**, -ere, tinxi, tinctum, vb. tr. *dip, dye*.

**tono**, -are, -ui, vb. intr. *thunder*.

**torrens**, torrentis, noun masc. *torrent*.

**tremo**, -ere, -ui, vb. tr. and intr. *tremble, shudder*.

**turbidus**, -a, -um, adj. *disturbed, boisterous*.

**turpis**, -e, adj. *hideous, disgraceful*.

**tūs**, tūris, noun neut. *incense*.

**ultimus**, -a, -um, adj. *furthest, last*.

**unda**, -ae, noun fem. *wave*, pl. *waters*.

**ūsus**, -us, noun masc. *use, need*.

**validus**, -a, -um, adj. *strong, mighty*.

**vallis**, -is, noun fem. *valley*.

**-ve**, coordinating conjunction, *or*.

**virgulta**, -orum, noun neut. plur. *thickets*.

**vīta**, -ae, noun fem. *life*.

# PROPER NAMES IN LIVY AND THE *OVID* EXTRACTS

*The few towns mentioned in the Livy chapters which are not to be found in the map of Western Central Italy are indicated by an asterisk.*

*The following are the abbreviations for the praenomina:*

| | |
|---|---|
| A. = Aulus. | M'. = Manius. |
| C. = Gaius. | P. = Publius. |
| Cn. = Gnaeus. | Q. = Quintus. |
| K. = Caeso. | Sp. = Spurius. |
| M. = Marcus. | T. = Titus. |

**T. Aebutius,** 19.

**Aequi,** -orum, a people N.E. of Rome, 20.

**Alba Longa,** a town in Latium, i.

**Albānus,** -a, -um, adj. to Alba Longa, 2.

**Ancus Marcius,** fourth king of Rome, 3.

**Apollo,** -inis, a Greek god, 9.

**Appius Claudius,** 20.

**Ardea,** a town of the Rutuli, 10.

**Arīcīnus,** adj. to Aricia, a town of Latium, 8.

**Aristodēmus,** 20.

**Arruns,** Arruntis, brother of Tarquinius Priscus, 3; son of Tarquinius Priscus, 7; son of Tarquinius Superbus, 9.

**Attius Tullius,** 21.

**Aurunci,** -orum, a people S.E. of Rome, 20.

**Caere,** an Etruscan city, 10.

**Capitōlīnus,** -a, -um, adj. to Capitolium, 9.

**Capitōlium,** -i, Capitoline hill, 15.

**Caprea,** i.

**Carmentālis,** -e, adj. to Carmentis, 24.

**Carmentis,** a Roman goddess, v.

**Sp. Cassius,** 21.

**Castor,** -oris, twin-brother of Pollux, 19.

**Cloelia,** -ae, 17.

*****Collātia,** -ae, a town in Latium, N.E. of Rome, 10.

*****Corinthus,** -i, a city in the Peloponnese, 3.

**Corioli,** -orum, a town in Latium, 21.

**Cremera,** -ae, a river in Etruria, 24.

*****Cūmae,** -arum, a seacoast town in Campania, 20.

**Cūriātii,** -orum, 2.

*Delphi, -orum, a city of Phocis, in Greece, where there was a famous oracle of Apollo, 9.

Etrūria, -ae, a large district of central Italy, 13.
Etruscus, -a, -um, adj. to Etruria, 8.

Fabia (gens), 23; Fabii: v. Caeso Fabius, M. Fabius, Q. Fabius, 23.
Ferentīna, -ae, a goddess. Aqua Ferentīna, a small river near Alba Longa, 8.

Gabii, -orum, a town in Latium, 10.

T. Herminius, 15.
Horātii, -orum, 2.
Horātius Cocles, 15.
M. Horātius Pulvillus, 14.

Iāniculum, -i, a hill on the remote side of the Tiber, 15.
Iānus, -i, arch, 24; temple of Janus, v.
Iūnius, -a, -um, adj. belonging to the Roman gens Iunia, 13.
L. Iūnius Brūtus, 9.
Iuppiter, Iovis, the king of the gods, 9.

Sp. Larcius, 15.
Lars Porsinna, 15.
Latīnus, -a, -um, adj. belonging to Latium, Latin, 3.
Laurens, -entis, adj. to Laurentum, a town of Latium, v.

Lāvīnium, -i, a town of Latium, 11.
Libycus, -a, -um, adj. Libyan, African, v.
Līvius, -i, 1.
Lucrētia, -ae, 10.
Sp. Lucrētius, 10.
Lucumo, -onis, 3.

Cn. Manlius, 23.
Cn. Marcius Coriolānus, 21.
Mars, Martis, god of war: warfare, v: issue of war, 3.
Menēnius Agrippa, 20.
C. Mūcius Scaevola, 16.

Numa Pompilius, second king of Rome, 1.

Octāvius Mamilius, 18.

Palātium,-i,Palatine hill,15.
Phoebus, -i, another name for Apollo, iii.
A. Postumius, 19.
Postumus Cominius, 21.
Proculus Iūlius, 1.

Quirīnus, -i, another name for Romulus, used after his deification, i.
Quirītes, -ium, Roman citizens, 14.

(Lacus) Regillus, a lake in Latium, 19.
Rōma, -ae, 1.
Rōmānus, -a, -um, adj. to Roma, 1.
Rōmulus, -i, first king of Rome, 1.
Rutuli, -orum, a people of Latium, 9.

**Sabīni**, -orum, a people N.E. of Rome, 20.

**Sacra Via**, a street in Rome, 17.

**P. Servīlius**, 20.

**Servius Tullius**, sixth king of Rome, 5.

**Sextus Tarquinius**, 10.

**Sicilia**, -ae, the island of Sicily, 21.

**(Pons) Sublicius**, a wooden bridge across the Tiber, 15.

**\*SuessaPōmētia**, a Volscian city, 9.

**Tanaquil**, 4.

**Tarquiniensis**, -e, adj. *belonging to Tarquinii*, 13.

**Tarquinius**, -a, -um, adj. *belonging to the Tarquins, Tarquinian*, 11.

**L. Tarquinius Collātīnus**, 10.

**L. Tarquinius Priscus**, fifth king of Rome, 4.

**L. Tarquinius Superbus**, seventh king of Rome, 7, 8.

**Tiberis**, -is, 5.

**Titus Tarquinius**, 9.

**Tullia maior**, 7.

**Tullia minor**, 7.

**Tullus Hostīlius**, third king of Rome, 2.

**Turnus**, -i, 8.

**Tusculānus**, -a, -um, adj. *belonging to Tusculum*, 19.

**Tusculum**, -i, a town in Latium, 18.

**Tuscus**, -a, -um, adj. *Etruscan*, 23.

**Tyrrhēnus**, -a, -um, adj. *Etruscan*, v.

**M'. Valerius**, 20.

**P. Valerius Publicola**, 10, 14.

**Veiens**, -entis, adj. *belonging to Veii*, an Etruscan city, 13.

**Velia**, -ae, a piece of high ground near the Palatine, 14.

**A. Verginius**, 20.

**Veturia**, -ae, 22.

**T. Veturius**, -i, 20.

**Volsci**, -orum, a people S. of Latium, 9.

**Volscus**, -a, -um, adj. *Volscian*, 21.

**Volumnia**, -ae, 22.

**Zephyrus**, -i, West wind, v.

9 780521 239486